ORGAN MUSIC

# ORGAN MUSIC

Jeff Hilson

Crater Press
61

Crater 61, The Crater Press, London
December 2020
ISBN: 978-1-716-54338-8

Cover image: *Gala Bingo Hall, Tooting* by Tim Atkins

20th Century was designed and drawn by Sol Hess in the Lanston Monotype drawing office between 1936 and 1947. The first weights were added to the Monotype typeface library in 1959. This is a face based on geometric shapes which originated in Germany in the early 1920s and became an integral part of the Bauhaus movement of that time.

Book design: Atkyns & Dottrs

And among all that we know of our history, the history of our organs and our organ music has been obscured.

Daniel Moult, The Elusive English Organ

FOREWORD

I began thinking about writing organ poems as far back as the early 1990s after reading an article in the Barbican Music Library about the recusant Catholic organ builder Robert Dallam* who fled England for Brittany with his family in 1642 because of persecution by the Puritans. Organs had been under threat in England as symbols of Popery since the 1540s, and in 1644 with the Parliamentary "Ordinance for the Further Demolishing of Monuments of Idolatry and Superstition," all organs were to be "taken away, and utterly defaced." This is one of the reasons there are so few early English organs left. If you're interested, watch the DVD by Daniel Moult called *The Elusive English Organ*.

Some years later I wrote a poem mentioning Dallam which I read out at the first Writers Forum workshop I attended, in late 1998 at The Victoria pub in Mornington Crescent. This, I think, was the last workshop held there as the upstairs 'reading' space was to be turned into a dining-only area to attract a more upmarket clientele than the workshop 'regulars.' Bob Cobbing soon found a new venue in Clerkenwell, another pub at the lower end of Mount Pleasant called The Churchill, before locating to the Betsy Trotwood near Farringdon which he continued to use for the workshops until his death in 2002.

It would perhaps be too much to forge a link between Dallam's decision to leave England and Cobbing's departure from The Victoria, although there's probably a connection to be made between Puritan vandalism and bourgeois gentrification – maybe the fact that as well as "utterly defacing" church organs, some Puritans removed them from places of worship and simply took them home. Either way, it was the Tory Party's election victory in 2010 and subsequent coalition government that became the impetus to begin *Organ Music* for real, and the 'longer' poems here are in their own way responses to ten years of the Tory regime which began with austerity and ended most recently with Brexit, with a whole lot more in between and, inevitably, to come. The shorter 'interludes' are little non-biographies, a good number of them referencing some of the key figures of early English music, composers and organists alike. These I envisioned as a kind of counterpoint to the longer sections or "sides" as I call them. I wanted to bring them right up to date, but with a few exceptions they barely make it out of the sixteenth century.

Halfway through, I stopped writing *Organ Music* and began another set of poems which became my book *Latanoprost Variations*, published by Boiler House Press back in 2017. I returned to *Organ Music* in 2018. Although there are obvious connections in places between the two books, because I left and then returned to it after some years *Organ Music* has (to my thinking anyway) something of an awkward 'brokeback' feel to it which I have now come to appreciate.

Somewhere recently I read how listening to the organ in church terrified a young John Lydon to the extent that he couldn't help but bring its frightening sounds to at least one of the PiL albums (I forget which one). Unlike Lydon, I recall sitting through Sunday mornings in the school chapel where the organ, along with hymn-singing, were all that made them bearable, the organ at the end of each service announcing a kind of temporary (though ultimately illusory) freedom. In his infamous essay on Bach, Theodor Adorno talks of the "acoustically static" character of the organ, I suppose because unlike the piano, organ dynamics are not principally a matter of touch. Perhaps Adorno was thinking more about the grand organs of mainland Europe rather than the smaller, more modest English instruments, pedal-less and with a single manual, which led in the late sixteenth century to the development of the 'voluntary,' that peculiarly English form of vibrant improvisation that 400 years later lifted my Sunday spirits.

In spite of the genius of the voluntary, it would perhaps be an overstatement to say that the traditional organ has ever gained a truly popular foothold in England, or more widely in Britain. Except to say that when David Bowie died in January 2016, some of the most unexpected tributes were the spontaneous organ renditions of "Life On Mars" by the organists of St Albans Cathedral and Glasgow's Kelvingrove Art Gallery, both of which became overnight social media sensations. Elsewhere I've argued that these renditions are a kind of 'dumbed-up' equivalent to the easy-listening tunes turned out by the great Hammond and Wersi maestros such as Klaus Wunderlich, Ethel Smith and Dick Hyman, 'the man from O.R.G.A.N.' You can find some of their records in the overlong notes and resources at the end of this book which are, if you like, evidence of research. In the process of writing, these resources have of course been transformed, though one might go further and say that they have been sabotaged, in Thorstein Veblen's sense of sabotage as "the conscious withdrawal of efficiency." Who wants to read an efficient poem? This might also be a tactic, as any fule kno [sic], against the smooth institutional "voluminous running administration of sabotage," presented as legitimate but whose workings Veblen rightly states are deliberately obscured by the more spectacular and occasional deployments of the term – a strike will always be noticed more than the call for research outputs or voluntary severance, those peculiarly recent English forms of improvised wordplay.

So, ultimately, this might not really be a book about the organ at all (a bit like bpNichol's *Organ Music*). It is partly about the organist, who in places in these poems I cast as an abject figure recalling the Fisher King in Eliot's *The Waste Land* who can't set his lands in order. One response to this would be, like Robert Dallam, to flee the country, and the various boats in these poems point to one means of escape. None of them are very effective. A scenario I imagined was floating down the river Quaggy past Lewisham's Shopping Centre and Street Market playing ancient protest songs to shoppers on a small portative organ on the way to Deptford Creek and out to the Thames. Only the Quaggy goes underground before reaching the Shopping Centre, running beneath Lewisham police station (the largest in Western Europe) before surfacing again briefly opposite the now-demolished Lewisham Odeon where David Bowie played in May 1973, two months before killing off Ziggy Stardust.

Everybody played the Lewisham Odeon – The Beatles, Little Richard, Tommy Roe, Stevie Wonder, Badfinger, Wings, Elf, The Kinks, Sparks, Siouxie Sioux, Squeeze, The Clash. In 1977 Status Quo played three nights in a row. No point playing there now – it would be Rock 'n' Roll Suicide. Elton John never played Lewisham, nor did Marvin Gaye, though he was photographed dancing in Cheeks nightclub down the road in Deptford in 1980, a few months before The Who played the final ever Lewisham Odeon gig in February 1981, as part of their *Face Dances* tour. Everyone knows you can't dance to The Who. Although originally subtitled "an antimasque not for dancing," you can dance to the poems in this book. Side 7 is a killer.

---

*Dallam's father, Thomas, travelled to Constantinople in 1599 to deliver a clockwork organ to the Ottoman Sultan Mehmet III, a gift from Queen Elizabeth I. Written up in his Diary, this forms the basis of the longer piece of poets theatre included here. In 2018 whilst on holiday, I visited the church of Ergué-Gabéric in Brittany to view one of the Dallam family organs (it's by Robert's son Thomas and *his* son Toussaint) but the church was closed. By all accounts it's a thing of wonder.

SIDE 1

I have broken more Elton John records, he seems to have a lot of records. And I, by the way, I don't have a musical instrument. I don't have a guitar or an organ. No organ.

Donald Trump, speaking at a Republican rally in Montana, July 2018

The second class of those practising music is that of the poets, a class led to song not so much by thought and reason as by a certain natural instinct. For this reason this class, too, is separated from music.

Boethius, De Institutione Musica

Good biz for cheapjacks, organs. What do ye lack?

James Joyce, Ulysses

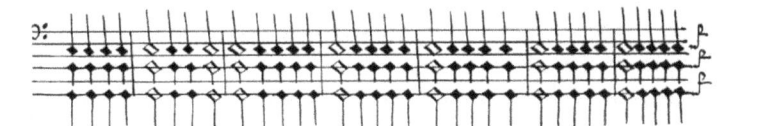

And I ran with my organ to the estuary
boy contra hautboy
I was already dreaming
of fountayne rd on the way in
tremulant   bourdon   gedackt
stopping to piss myself
in my pants & ting
I picked up the voluntary at crouch-roach
& rother & dengie & can
in my pants & ting I am obviously still listening
no I am not fishing
I am listening & playing
the organs of england

its not easy being a fancy organist
in uncertain time
I just start off on the portative
slow quick slow really
I am such a silly bee
(it was a time when silly bees could speak)
buzzing in & out of the water
slender & shutmouthed
but the showiest commonest most widespread
bee

today I am playing st-peter-on-the-wall
today I am playing principal
today I am playing bullwood hall

the bees come & go I dont notice them
widespread is the pussy willow
in this book I will be mainly crying
in distracted time
the mr men are everywhere partying like its
1649
but I am not in this together with you
I dont know why the mr men
he broke my organ
the mr men says
I dont know how to play the organs
the mr men says
a angel can hold a organ in one hand
I see it in bermondsey & when I'm walking
always talking shit
in the fields of south london
but mr men I am serious
we must begin with the quaggy

& I ran with my organ to the quaggy
(mr men he dead in a thorn wood)
today I am playing *trompette militaire*
toot! toot!
its not unusual to be free & loud
bill I'm very sorry about this bill
the clouds/move sometimes/away from/the sun
& when no one was looking
I made the english organ out of grass
& a boat out of my thumb
& a anchor in my image
& all who sail with me on the quaggy
when no one was looking
I lay down in a box
in my khaki suit and ting
just to listen to the air going out & in

& floating to france with dr john
we are already sick of musica
britannica when we went down in *spartina*
anglica & danced an image
of melancholy there
I like to dance so much & a kind of mania
make me wind up my waist
to the english keyboard tradition
o *spartina anglica* I think
the world is ready for a novum *novum organum*
where I am the dr & the admiral &
I *are* yr missing winner
beginning all over the place
in the present crisis
my pipes are narrow & small
in the kingdom of teares
I am floating to france with elton john
& not dr john I think
the world is not ready for *lachrymae novae novae*
when I go down
with my dancing master
to the sea in ships
it is full of the holes
of john blow there are so many
johns in the seventeenth century
I never actually met
john blow I am lost again
in the windy channel everyone is talking
about my khaki suit I am sinking
in my heels & ting I am
a shit admiral with my organs in
the lock up garages of SE13
they are dark garages full of the english
going into battle with mr silly
I dont know which side is best side

one of captain fantastic
or side two

the organ in england
its very windy with strong men
always opening and closing
as strong as the bishop of winchester who
suddenly is 1406 &
it is the christmas party
& suddenly it is chaucers birthday &
& it is 1649
william byrd is dead
thomas tomkins is dead
(who is hugh facy who suddenly dies?)
& for a long time henry purcell shaketh
(it is after all now the seventeenth century)
scarlatti is finished
& germany is waiting
& american poetry is everywhere
& its just the speed
the speed of bachs hands

SIDE 2

listening to music, my misery, that's why I want to sing.

Allen Ginsberg, "Transcription of Organ Music"

And even though the stars are listening
And the ocean's deep, I just go to sleep...

Supertramp, "Even in the Quietest Moments"

What of the world's sleepers?
What harm comes of them,
while the organ dusts and silts in its ranks.

Bill Griffiths, "Morning Lands"

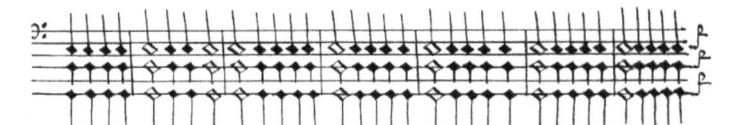

O bill I bought a twister I never
had so much fun either
the unexpected
strawberry fruit ice core
are you lonely in your boat
what I mean is I am
the organ in england is too
is too big for my room
I am always going to the seaside
to shake up the nation
in my big empty room it is always 1979
in my big empty nation I
fucking loved you supertramp
theres no room in my boat
for this rough music I never left
the room where really I am listening
to the organ rarely listening to it
on my boat or galley or sometimes raft
& even in the quietest moments
I hate my quiet tits
but I fucking loved breakfast
in america I wish I was american
take a look at my quiet tits I wouldnt
play the organ or anymore
fancy english girl organists
even their records nobody loves
english girls not even supertramp o
I wouldnt carry on so
if I was an american organist

about how my tits
in the quiet english countryside are
really silly anglo american relations

I will never make it in the atlantic ocean
the invading english organ is too small
& without any pedals
I am standing on the bridge
of hms new british poetry
& sailing to america when I went down
without any medals
when I was admiral
I cant even read without launching
a thousand poems
without laughing
& manoeuvring with difficulty
now I am a boy organist
I cant even read music
when I was a girl on the mutiny on the bunty
with a list of the english men of war
I mean to carry on all night
I have a motor boat I have no motor boat
my position is doubtful I have collided
with your present crisis
the present crisis I have collided with
is on fire
the fire is in the engine room
where is the fire
the fire is in the boiler room
I am on fire amid ships
are you aground no I am on fire
on what ground have you gone aground on
no I am on fire aft
you are bunkers
I expect I am bunkers

it is likely you are bunkers
yes I am bunkers

A 1ST ABC OF STOPS

assat
bifara
chalumeau
drums
english horn
fagotto
glockenton
harp
jeu érard
keraulophone
larigot
montre
nineteenth
ophicleide
piffero
quint
racket
schlangenrohr
tenoroon
unda maris
vox angelica
wienerflöte
xylophone
zink

INTERLUDE...

knock knock whos there john dowlands/
why john dowlands you look rough/
rough in the ruff that youre rough in/
o john dowlands we love your get up/
comely john dowlands first among
the evergreens/now he is stalking me
in my chamber/go away from my window/
go john dowlands go/both your hands sound
ridiculous/the king of spain is uninteresting
in your ingrown arms/ho ho john dowlands
the lights are on/very likely this year you
will not come again in your triumph/in his
triumph quickly john dowlands drives
through the continental lowlands/he is ornate
at taverners party he is longer than his long
lute/in his triumph quickly john dowlands
drives through the continental ploughlands/
john dowlands why the long lute/ho ho
homely john dowlands/ho ho lonely john
dowlands

SIDE 3

Construe my meaning, wrest not my method.

Giles Farnaby, "Construe My Meaning"

Zwei Hände zaubern ein Orchester.

Klaus Wunderlich, The Sensational Organ Sound of Klaus Wunderlich

Organs, organs, organs, organs,
Organs in cassocks and organs in uniforms,
Organs, organs, organs, organs,
Organs, organs, organs in uniforms.

Pussy Riot, "Organy"

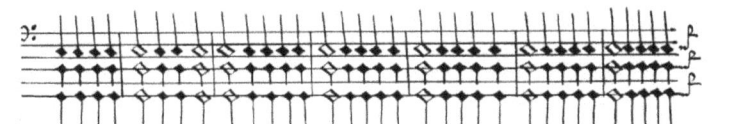

In any english year it doesnt matter
if I'm always playing outside
like a midsummer man
like a medicine man
lifting women & lifting men
when I was a cuckoo
loving my other name & giving it
to the pretty bird in may I didnt think
I was the only cuckoo bird
I didnt think anyone is actually listening
to my long playing records
now its june I'm playing something else
& getting very dainty in the arena

ut re mi

its nobodys gig bonjour mon coeur
the rose queen is dead in farnabys dream
she's singing a song for anything of the dead
for the girls in farnabys dream
I come sweet birds
magnificat sexy tony-de-la-court

ut re mi fa

o ye tender babes
sexy tony is giving you ear
o tony give ear
day after day thy magnificat ears

o christ tony thou hast cut us off dis
courteously
for the girls in farnabys dream
was my delight
now my ears are bursting forth err
onerously

ut re mi fa sol

my magnificat embarrassing body of work
is all my joy
its called o god its greensleeves playing fer
ociously
in every tree who broke thy music
miserere tony-de-la-coeur
when I was a nightingale
night after night my miserere opus
is everywhere in the pines

ut re mi fa sol la

dont look now I think the pontiff is coming
I want to play for him full without the trumpet

clangorem   longius   resonantem

he's getting into my long forgotten boat
the babbling pontiff isnt strong enough
since he's italian since he's a gemini
I dont want to play for him
he's still talking
theoretically
he's a venetian
its likely he's looking to enlarge his organ
oh dear he's wearing a crown

& touching my head &
pulling & pushing it & because of an error
I have flown with the pontiff to tenerife
who loves the law & order there . . .

I love the rugged coastline . . .

he loves the law & order &
the cathedral of la laguna

. . . I love the buses & trams . . .

he loves the holiday of
the virgin of candelaris

. . . I love the air quality &
the playa de las americas . . .

he loves the church of our
lady of los remedios

. . . I love the nightlife here I am
entering disco big ben . . .

he loves the spanish conquest
& the british invasion

. . . I love dick hyman & the semi
quaver runs of rod hunter . . .

he loves the pilgrimage
of mary of the head

. . . I just love embroidery
& flags & heraldry

caballas & chicharros
& patatas arrugadas
& I am always kissing
him who I love who loves
the law & order
I stole his clothes its so cold
on the ferry where
I am going
is where I am going
far?

INTERLUDE...

why john dunstaple I hardly know you/
can I borrow your memorable face/your
english countenance is quite quite rare/o
constaple I have fallen for john/john
dunstaple/in the 1440s he is very forward/
he is finished with gloria & he is finished
with carol/& I am finished with john
dunstaple/o god we are all plantagenets/
a tudor is neither male nor female/whoever
is besieging the house of carpets/nobody
painted their burgundian kitchen/why
john dunstaple why/because I was
in my coat of arms in the burning house
of windsor/embattled & dancetty
I left my shield in your ordinary extra
field/& I lied in the ground in wavy armour/
& I lied in the ground of eton college/
& I lied in the ground in armed corsets/
& I lied in the ground on dunstaple downs

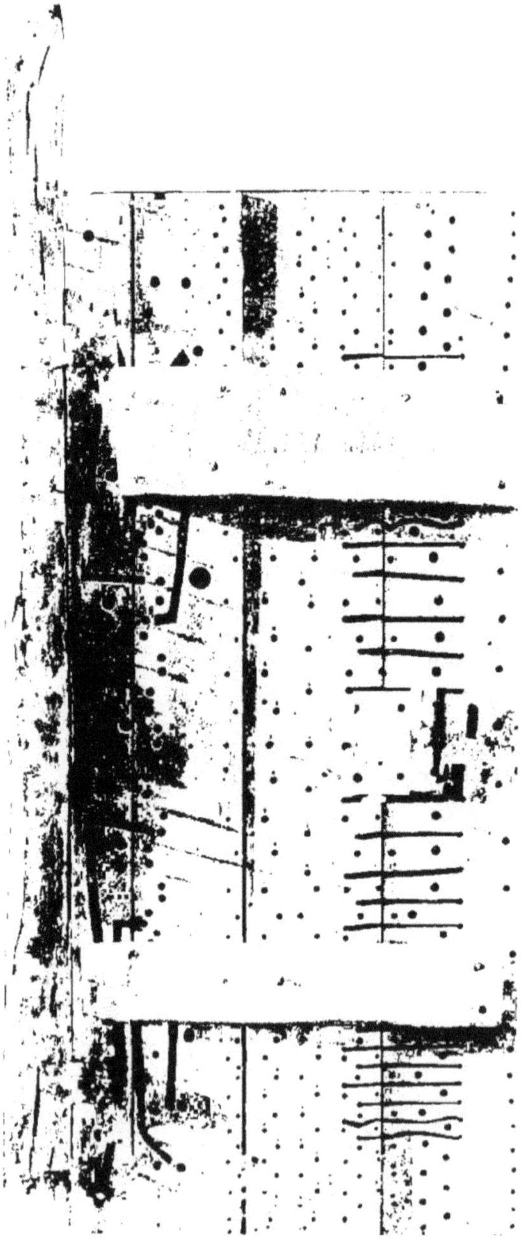

PLAY FOR TODAY

[*A farmhouse dairy in the town of Wetheringsett, Suffolk. The dairy door swings gently in the breeze.*]

DOOR: I wasnt always a door.

[Enter the MILKMAID.]

MILKMAID: A talking door.

DOOR: I am full of holes.

MILKMAID: Woodworm.

DOOR: I am full of the holes of John Blow.

MILKMAID: Wormwood.

DOOR: When a door is not a door...

MILKMAID: Wormrow.

DOOR: ...it is a tiny dancer.

MILKMAID: Hold me closer tiny dancer...

DOOR: Tiny dancer in my hand...

MILKMAID: Lay me down in sheets of linen...

[*The door and the milkmaid continue singing Elton John's "Tiny Dancer" until Bob Cobbing dies.*]

THE END

Note on the above: In 1977, five years after the release of Elton John's "Tiny Dancer," and during the restoration of an old East Anglian farmhouse, the dairy door — pocked and groovy — was discovered to be the soundboard of a rare pre-Reformation English organ.

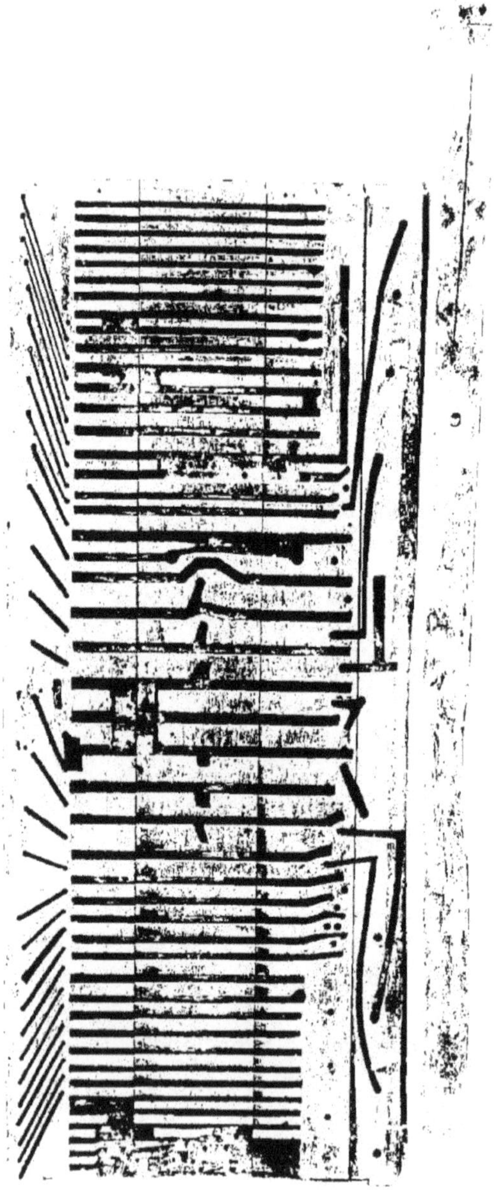

SIDE 4

Britain is nothing now, Britain is fuck all, my Britain is fuck all now, fuck all, my British is fuck all.

Emma West, aka "Tram Lady"

Listen, and for organ music thou wilt ever, as of old, hear the Morning Stars sing together.

Thomas Carlyle, Sartor Resartus

ma someone is spoiling this scenario.

Hannah Weiner, "We Speak Silent"

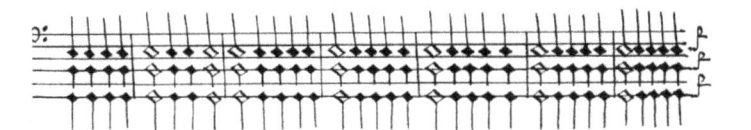

As a grammatical person
I mean as a first person organist
& here are the congregation going out
& in the wrong way round
I am always going in
& out of focus
like who is going to do my housework
now the congregation are striking
dont ask me when I'm playing hard
to smack the congregation up
the congregation are mental when I'm hoovering
always going out & in
instead I wish they would agree
to do my housework
in my homework
I am learning about the ancien régime
"in his noble robes the frondman"
o hyacinth! o couperin!
the unexpected valois are succeeding
& passing through
the house of carpets
meanwhile the bourbons are broken
& because of my homework
the congregation are rioting
I wish they would agree to do my housework
at least they are rioting correctly
inexhausto   tempestate   furiaeque

if I was a rioter
but I am only the organist
who smashed up the bourbons
& the cops are the following
the cops are the following me
the english girl in the congregation
who smashed up the bourbons
who are fighting me on the beaches
are the broken bourbons
I will never surrender
my ladye nevells booke of hand to hand combat
sometimes it feels like yip man camp
everybody wing chun tonight
these deadly wrists
the secret grips of japan

& the cops are all norsemen
in my ragamuffin arms
the agency organist of the tottenham attack
o ladye I cannot stand it here
where I am a racist
go home brian eno
here come the chinese keyboardists
with your great white heart
in my yellow van
goodbye barry rose
in thy millennium stadium
instead of fixing it o ladye
I am filling it with poems for the millennium
anyone can look inside
my massive book of johnson & johnson fun
where ladye your body perspires

not just under the armour
whose ronald johnson legs
I am tired of fighting for
& lubriderm eyes
see no one is opposing
the terracotta strongmen
the golden trunks of strongman no. 5
the no. 7 strongman his copper tripod
& b.s. johnson is holding up
the british museum
when I unfriended the emperor
the tiny boots of his dynasty organists
are making me cry
& kissing my ladyes fingers
because she gives me ears
as well as tongues
o my terracotta ladye
because we have tongues
as well as
fingers & softer
than dumplings the swell ancilliaries
of wendi deng
I only go to iceland wendi
with the other mothers
to pick up common moms
aisles full of moms
my mom is beside me in the frozen light
she's my mom my
common mom says thats why
moms go to iceland
my common mom says
all of the organists are dead

& my british is fuck all wendi
who in my country have gone to specsavers
to look at the beautiful beautiful beautiful
tram of moms who
o ladye of the tram just like you
will be your british & country
organist & congregation
common mom tram slag

sorry about that I am only the organist
& tram driver &/or military
wife singing I wanted
with my other voice
to obviously fistfuck gareth malone
loveable gareth malone
& then &/or his mom
for xmas in your nation
in your car I mean
in your xmas choir when he came out
driving you wherever you are
with his no. 1 single choirmaster
small conducting arm
& with the other wives obviously
I wanted to fistfuck affable gareth malone
& with all my voices
in his home alone
& then &/or his mom
when I was your wife I dreamed I shot arrows
in my gareth malone bra
arrows of outrageous desire
outrageous unfolding army surplus bras
I dreamed of fistfucking national gareth malone in

it was no dream gareth malone having flown

over & over
my strong organist hands
when the music stopped all the wives came
to england
to look at the poetry wars
why gareth malone I hardly know you
meanwhile
all the kandehar girls go vox *inaudita*
exploded by the congregation
you lived your life like I
really am distantly other
over
like I really am distantly mother

A 2ND ABC OF STOPS

anthropoglossa
bombarde
cinq
diapason
echo oboe
fife
gedecktbommer
hautboy
jula
koppel
lute
majorbass
nachthorn
oboe
pauke
querflöte
reim
sackbut
twelfth
untersatz
vox humana
waldhorn
zartgedeckt

INTERLUDE...

to all the single ladies of polyphony
so long/tallys is dead o christ shoulder
to shoulder into the streets who f'umth/
I f'umth you f'umth he she or it f'umth/
do we o joan in raging stout syllable to
syllable/please drive slowly music is dying
& I am dissolving/doctor doctor I think
I am an english tudor organist not really
you are just an american poet not really
I am henry the eighth without organs/
am I joan retallack/are you whose voce *flebile*
did this to me in your fortypart motel
stop doing that in a minute o happy man/
did you think I am archbishop parker
all over myself & the pissy boys I dont
even like thomas tallys on my face without
music on/but I love the pissy boys going
my way/now in the mouth/again joan/o
mine eyes//f'umth/f'umth

INTERLUDE...

in my orlando gibbons fantasy go glenn
gould & do not whack the circlebearded
boys of the lord of salisbury/going glenn
gould straight returned virginal & un-
organistic/feminine the endings of henrietta
maria heretofore her kittens thereupon
marie antoinette/in the beginning orlando
gibbons came forth rallying glenn
gould in idiot mittens like the boys of the lord
of salisbury in furious ermine jerking in
thy wrath I'm sorry I cut off your boyhands
of ancient origin/only honourable men
go with honourable men with arms playing
renaissance tag up & down your silent moog/
o god I'm it or orlando gibbons or the lord
of salisbury is it from whose boys glenn
gould hies via o canada of a roomful of spies/
gee farewell jerks hello sighs/of the boyhands
of the boybands ancient or modern or revised

INTERLUDE...

to be bolder oftener than any expected
john/john who with bold splashes splashes
solo off & on & answers no or yes/oh no
john no/answer do I'm all crazy over half
of you nearly the other half of me is going
sincerely/all I need is a great big metaphor
to kneel down in like the tower of hamlets/
really bold/really old/older oftener than
john ashbery expected john ashbery or un
expected joan of gaunt which came first/
enter joan of gaunt quick or dead exit john
ashbery bigger than thy head/enter john
bull by force chopping down the goddam
big tower of hamlets instead/which was not
the same/really I want to be any john who
had me together in his carriage as bold as
john of malmesbury/arise sir john one by
one out of the useless past sir joan arose
& out of any useless arc

SIDE 5

Owre kynge went forth to Normandy,
With grace and myyt of chivalry;
The God for hym wrouyt marvelously,
Wherefore Englonde may calle, and cry...

Anon, "The Agincourt Carol"

Lifesaver, doughnut, onion ring, or halo;
Lacuna, vacuum, emptiness, or hole—
The UFOs in Limbo hover way low;
In Purgatory, langue's denied parole.

K. Silem Mohammad, from SONNAGRAMS

Until he'd seen which Captain You said
He'd seen nothing.

Alice Notley, 165 Meeting House Lane

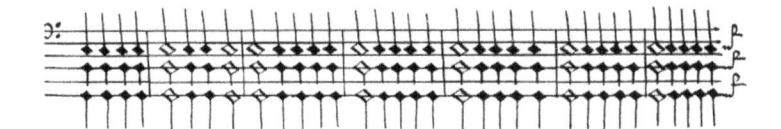

Susi runs slightly small marie-claire doesnt know her english shoe size jennifer has an awayday feeling about her footwear not like gillian slow at home in mary janes also her way across the pedalboard is bold her span style bold her accidentals oh carol I will surely die untouched me & the beautiful interrupters like when I was in agincourt it felt like I already was mr england me & the beautiful runner ups no mr england I am not like you & your tiny swimmers I am very strictly mr november who the door must be closed on in the hours when captain poetry dark flowers on my head & makes me light & glad which the beautiful runner ups always requires who are not like you mr england & your tiny winners they are the second place finishers running up or interrupting in gory agincourt it doesnt matter which joan plays the organ while we carry on in agincourt its so confusing the field of battle & the field of play are both fields but the poem is a dark fighting flower I ran away from in a transport of joy please dont tear me apart I would be an anchoress instead of the duke of bedford in a scholarly trap when three transports came along at once all shall be well & all shall be well & all manner of thing shall be well you couldnt make it up the longbowmen are not using realistic arrows at grisly agincourt the slaughter of the constables of france with fake english weaponry is almost a fanatical joy for me & joan who are changing in the field out of our bombsuits & into our hellbunnies its not easy being a made up longbowman the arrows go right through instead of the maid of kent I wish I was a tudor rose playing the voluntary for double organ in d minor by henry purcell two hundred and fifty years too early at girly agincourt really listening rarely listening to it when the interrupters all ran away stop all manner of thing is not well the poem are not a dark fighting flower after all it are a speed garage compilation of the toughest anthems o rosie just when I am getting closer to my uncontrollable desire I am closer than I thought now I've gone too far I wanted you in my karaoke masterclass where I am crying like at the end of toy story three where old time and new time are really the same time & andy is also crying because he is going further than me into the future with mr cuddles stop all manner of thing is not well the voluntary for double organ in d minor are broken & susi & marie-claire & jennifer & gillian are aliens singing to me every time I hear them combining their khaki hair they capture my pea green boat they are not pirates they are not aliens I am not even a pussycat they are just a fancy organist please dont marry me I am sailing away on the cruiser the pinky paper it is only a research vessel I also carry divers & plenty of money for the pirates & for the aliens & for the fancy organist look at their dazzle ships where no one can see them capturing me & killing me with here & there a cor damour & a cor glorieux & anyway all manner of rayguns & now I am small & dying & having a fantastic voyage in their dazzle ships hither & thither into the hadron era it didnt last I hardly collided with anyone from the avantgarde into the inflationary epoch where everything begins with z even the ABC in sound in & out of it tripping on the big rip in & out of nebulous dawn during the late heavy bombardment I dreamed of a mother ship old & new THE CHASEY MOHAMMAD

everything begins with head you said in sci-fi all the fancy organists are dead & susi & marie-claire & jennifer & gillian are having the best time at the party I'm just having the milkiest way in space some organists believe that nobody can hear you otrireme on & off the handymax on & off THE CHASEY MOHAMMAD o yes I do at moments like these fire arrows at your hysteron proteron I wish I had my flarfgun set to force hyperbaton I wish I had my flarfgun set to me

INTERLUDE...

now we are all ruck positive or amoroso
or bombarde en chamade/sounding the
parley everybody sank their jollyboats/
aye-aye in the beginning she leadeth me
overboard with maximum pedals down
to her ships of eve/avast the sloops-of-war/
abandonships all ye who spied her tutti
indicators/turning them over & her row
row boats of awe/over her pianoforte over/
over her pissharmonica the boy seaman &
the men of coventry ahoy/here she comes
is she coming quietly or full of noise/
cro orlo cro orlo go the eyes of the men
of coventry/wandering eyes/the wandering
hands of men inland/whole cities looking
at her galleys going/looking at her galleons
gone/tarantantara goes the coventryman
at the wives of the men-of-war/goes my life/
goes my wife

THOMAS DALLAM – A TRAGICOMEDY OF ORIGINAL SPELLING IN THREE ACTS

Act 1, Scene 1 – Gravesend

[*It is 1599. Enter the celebrated Renaissance organ builder THOMAS DALLAM, downcast & sighing. He is preparing to leave for the Levant to deliver a pipe organ, a gift from QUEEN ELIZABETH I, to the Sultan of the Ottoman Empire.*]

DALLAM: For my voyage into Turkie I have no frend to advise me in any thinge…

[*Enter QUEEN ELIZABETH I with items for Dallam's voyage.*]

QUEEN: Item one sute of sackcloth.

DALLAM (*sighing*): another sute.

QUEEN: Item three shirtes.

DALLAM (*sighing*): three shirtes more.

QUEEN: a pare of virginals.

DALLAM:) a pare of virginals!

[*He places the virginals on board HMS Hector. Exit QUEEN. Enter the CAPTAINE OF THE SHIPPE who is also bound by Sixteenth Century orthography.*]

CAPTAINE: Anker is wayed!

[*Exit the CAPTAINE OF THE SHIPPE.*]

DALLAM (*sighing*): I forgot my fustion britches.

[*Exit DALLAM*]

Scene 2 – In the English Channel

[*Sodonly a marvalus storme. Enter DALLAM*]

DALLAM: (*sodon*) We did not only louse our pinis we lost our selves.

[*finding themselves again.*]

We found our selves than we founde our pinis!

[*Trumpet sounds. Enter the CAPTAINE OF THE SHIPPE.*]

CAPTAINE: No, only our pinis.

DALLAM: We could spare the pinis.

[*Enter MEN OF WAR.*]

CAPTAINE (*assaying the MEN OF WAR*): Com the more bouldly upon us.

MEN OF WAR (*ignoring him*): Com under our Lee side.

CAPTAINE: See the stoutnes of our ship.

MEN OF WAR: Flye away!

[*The CAPTAINE gives chase.*]

MEN OF WAR: We have almost loste sighte of our pinis.

CAPTAINE: Com into my cabbin.

MEN OF WAR (*unwillingly*): We woll, we woll (*by their speech, Dutchmen*).

We are all Amberalls, rear Amberalls & wise Amberalls.

CAPTAINE: You speake good Inglishe.

MEN OF WAR: Let our shippes go. We are nothinge but men.

CAPTAINE (*striding upon the spar deck*): You are all a goner.

[*Drawing his sword he kills the MEN OF WAR.*]

I am becalmed.

DALLAM: Onwards to Barberie!

[Exit DALLAM & THE CAPTAINE OF THE SHIPPE.]

Scene 3 – Reaching Algiers

[Enter DALLAM and his new fainthearted friend MYGHELL WATSON THE JOINER.]

DALLAM: It Lyethe close to the seae.

MYGHELL WATSON THE JOINER: They have a great store of hens & chickins.

DALLAM: Great store of partridgis & quales.

MYGHELL WATSON THE JOINER: Great store of corne & frute.

DALLAM: Great store of hote houses.

MYGHELL WATSON THE JOINER: Greate store of Camels.

DALLAM: & som dromedaries.

MYGHELL WATSON THE JOINER: Thar be a greate number of Turks.

DALLAM: Both wylde & tame.

MYGHELL WATSON THE JOINER: & verrie relidgus.

DALLAM: The weomen goo with there facis covered & have no souls.

MYGHELL WATSON THE JOINER (seeing a snake in a tree): A great Ader. He is even Reddie to leape upon us!

[MYGHELL WATSON THE JOINER runs into a thicket of briars.]

DALLAM (turning to the audience): A number of other suche smale matters I will omitte.

[*Exit DALLAM.*]

Act 2, Scene 1 — Entering the Dardanelles

[*Enter DALLAM.*]

DALLAM: The Dardanelles. And look, the wals of Troye.

[*HMS Hector is met by the Turkish navy.*]

DALLAM: Ha Ha their sailes are made of cotton woll!

[*The Turkish navy fires its guns.*]

And so neare the wals of Troy! The eckco. The eckco.

[*Exit DALLAM carrying off a marble pillar from the Trojan ruins which he takes to The British Museum.*]

Scene 2

[*After many months at sea, HMS Hector weighs anchor in Constantinople.
Enter DALLAM who must now attend to the serious business of constructing his organ.*]

DALLAM: Open our chestes.

[*Enter unexpectedly the exiled KING OF FEZ whose country has been annexed by the Emperor of Morocco. The situation is complex.*]

THE KING OF FEZ (*looking into the first opened chest*): All the glewinge worke is clene Decayed!

DALLAM (*looking into another chest*): My mettle pipes are brused and broken!

THE KING OF FEZ: It is not worth iid.

Scene 3

[*Enter DALLAM who has much work to do restoring his organ after the months at sea. Thirty days later it is ready to present to the Sultan of the Ottoman Empire or, as he is known in 1599, THE GRAND SINYOR.*]

[*Enter first the ENGLISH AMBASSADOR.*]

AMBASSADOR: Yow are come hether wythe a presente from our gratious Quene?

DALLAM: I am.

AMBASSADOR: The monarch is an infidell (*meaning the Grand Sinyor, not the Quene*). He is a myghtie monarch of the world and you must kiss his kne or hanginge sleve.

DALLAM: ffs.

AMBASSADOR: If your organ doo not please him at the first sighte and perform not those thinges which it is Toulde him that it can Dow he will cause it to be puled downe that he may trample it under his feete.

[*pause*]

Hee strangled all his brotheres.

[*pause*]

DALLAM: OK I will come with my mate Harvie. He is an ingineer.

[*Exit DALLAM & the ENGLISH AMBASSADOR. Enter DALLAM an hour or two later...*]

I have sett my worke in good order. Here is the Grand Sinyor cominge upon the water.

Act 3, Scene 1

[Enter THE GRAND SINYOR in his golden caique & THE SULTANA his mother, in like manner.]

THE SULTANA: I doe not speake.

[she is anyway thinking of the visit to her garden earlier that day by the English Ambassador's dreamy secretary Paule Pinder.]

THE GRAND SINYOR: Silence!

[The organ plays. It is equipped with a clock which strikes twenty-two. Then a bell chimes sixteen times and it plays a four part song.]

It is good.

[Two clockwork trumpeters on each corner sound a tantarara after which the organ plays a five part song twice over.]

I wonder at its divers motions.

[The whole edifice is topped by a holly bush full of blackbirds & thrushes which at the end of the music sing and shake their wings.]

Will it goo at any time?

DALLAM: It will goo at any time if you tuche this pin with your finger.

[long pause]

THE GRAND SINYOR: Lett me se you playe on the orgon.

DALLAM: I have a wyfe and Childrin in Inglande. Do not cut of my heade.

THE GRAND SINYOR: I wil give you fourtie five peecis of gould and tow wyfes either of my Concubines or els tow virgins.

[He shows him his CONCUBINES through a grate in the wall.]

CONCUBINES (through the grate): Wee doe not speake.

DALLAM: At first sighte of them I thought they had bene yonge men and verrie prettie ones in deede.

THE GRAND SINYOR: They are weomen.

DALLAM: Yes & the hare of their heads hange doone on their backs...

THE GRAND SINYOR: In deede.

DALLAM: ...a juell hanging on each breast...

THE GRAND SINYOR: ...& juels in their ears...

DALLAM: In deede.

THE GRAND SINYOR: They are wearing britches of fine coton clothe...

DALLAM (*thinking wistfully of his own pair in London*): ...as fine as muslin & whyte as snow...

THE GRAND SINYOR: In deede.

DALLAM: I can disorne the skin of their thies through it...

(*Looking long on them*) ...som of their leges are naked...

THE GRAND SINYOR (*stamping his feet*): My kindnes begins to be verrie anger. Give over looking!

DALLAM: I am loth to give over the sighte does please me wondrous well...

[page missing]

EDWARD SAID: Run for your wife!

DALLAM (*putting on new shoues*)

[page missing]

MYGHELL WATSON THE JOINER: They have hewed me all in peecis!

[page missing]

Scene 3 — Dover

(Enter DALLAM, MY MATE HARVIE, MYGHELL WATSON THE JOINER & THE MEN OF KENT.]

DALLAM: I am verrie glad we are once againe upon Inglishe ground.

MY MATE HARVIE: Sound the trompetes!

MYGHELL WATSON THE JOINER (limping): Make our selves as merrie as we can.

THE MEN OF KENT: Post horse to Canterburrie.

MY MATE HARVIE: And thenc to Rochester.

DALLAM: And the nexte day to London (he is thinking only of his fustian, a type of cloth believed to have originated in 2nd Century AD Egypt).

THE END

SIDE 6

I am the Head, and it is my Body.

King James I, Speech to Parliament, 19 March, 1604

But I gotta guard the head.
Don't you see?
Who'll keep the head?

Bill Griffiths, "A Tale of a Head"

Chip chop chip chop the last man is dead.

Anon, "Oranges and Lemons"

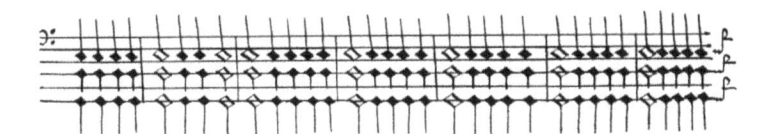

The english organ is very quiet today I cant hardly bear it instead of playing oranges & lemons girls & boys the legs of the men of war are going inside & out inside & out & all in a row carrying their big new head it grew so big they had to cut it off now they are carrying it to something beginning with zed inside & out inside & out you mustnt wake the head or it will kill you like the bells of st clements chop chop & when the wind changed I stayed that way waiting all day for the head to come home I only wanted to kiss the head and clap it I am only waiting for my turn to clap its me next I said I nearly presented my arms I began to clap so hard I nearly woke up the head I cant wait to carry on presenting my arms all by myself clap clap like the great bell of bow all in a row clap clap & then we found out a head is forever & not just for turning left or right or for looking at france & I have to take my hat off I didnt know I have to take off so many hats just to present my arms hundreds & thousands of hats who wants them do you o men of war I dont know you ye know now I am taking off my armour quietly hear my prayer first the left leg then the right normally is blown off hundreds & thousands of legs going up to heaven saying unto me they are only legs theres no such thing as legs but I was wrong every leg is born again clap clap say the bells of st clements & really the bells were clapping my legs as they freely descended one by one onto the gardens of england I even cried I dont want any legs today but the bells never listen to you when theyre clapping some bells even cheer when somebody says its ok to have something beginning with a leg or a name like the great bell of bow I dont want a name neither said the bell dont clap when you see your name all in a row or say your name when the wind changes it didnt mean the head changes like a name or a flag a flag only goes up or down like a name you cant have half a name even if you cut it in half like a flag of convenience said the bells of st clements or a flag of legs waiting for its turn to flap up & down all by itself flap flap first the left then the right normally is convenient hundreds & thousands of oranges & lemons but really only one flag by itself shaking like me its afraid its going to be used today instead of clapping my daddy is shaking like me my daddy is wrong I even cried I dont want a daddy like me ye know I want a man of war daddy with realistic arms even two man of war daddies are bad girls & boys if they fall in love if they fall in a river they are wet thats right even two man of war daddies with gripping hands are wet after a storm wet & then dry like a flag this time a false flag I once was sitting next to when one of us forgot about the true meaning of the head knock knock it goes against the door it wants to be a hand when its only a head knock knock whos there the head who the same head as before I am the head it said & its my head & on the way up all I can see is hats of war falling everywhere a head is no good without a hat it flops about flop flop or bangs about bang bang without a hat a head of war is just like any other head a hard luck head or a head of many colours which are not real heads like a blown off head going round & round the garden & when the wind changed it isnt a head its just something beginning with head its just a head of hair talking I fell in love with which isnt real love I loved it when the head of hair said you cant eat my heart out &

theres no such thing as hearts & so on & so on until the bells stopped & the organ started the english organ & the big new head in the night time woke me up & killed me with its little eye

written on the day of the Thatcher funeral April 17 2013

A 3RD ABC OF STOPS

amorosa
bassonell
carillon
duophone
engelstimme
fiffaro
german gamba
hörnlein
junfernregal
kinura
litice
melodia
nason
orlo
phocinx
quintenbass
regal
serpent
tromba
voix éolienne
weidenpfeife
zauberflöte

INTERLUDE...

again I lost my nerve to tristitia et anxietas/
both are overtaking me on the inside I
am a vigilante like little bob maximus who
on the outside had a little dog/o william
byrd where are you going on the inside today
I wrote nothing/sometimes in the tudors I
play norfolk sometimes I play shrewsbury
I never play throckmorton who is my rival/
christ I am rising again in a miniseries & am
going to die/throckmorton is my rival/the knights
of mendoza are taking me from both sides the
knights of mendoza take hours to kill/o william
byrd where is your unidentified country horse/
on the outside I am not a madrigalian no
one likes mary queen of scots her hands are
one thousand two thousand three thousand
years old & must still be washed/I am still
killing mendozas knights/throckmorton is
dead/its senselessness/the little dog

INTERLUDE...

now I am dismissed by christopher tye/
farewell my good I my other I is dumb my
dumb ears & nose & throat doctor said
jesus chris/pa rum pum pum pum/in a
way I bet you look good in a manger or
toiling near the earth/touching my harp
of gold I was only saying if only I hadnt
when I spake thus about your organs of
corti with such sh-sh-shaky hands played
my drum for you/for dr tye who is out
of tune is out of time & hurting me like/
ouch/the book of smackes or/ouch/the
smackes of the apostles/I was only playing
for them my drum when they broke thus
my stickes now I am dismissed & *together
they into* me *dyd cum*/pa rum pum pum pum/
oh dr tye/who are not listening/its not xmas
why am I on my knees my otolaryngologist
never does say say ah or cheese

INTERLUDE...

its february & all the tudor organists are
weeping oh jeff I love you too but the
farmers on my land have wives of their own
how can I make it work a fucking tractor
only needs a little push/shush the organists
are sleeping & dreaming of poetry/I still
cant get no tractor to go backward at a cater
pillar factory its so slow a cater pillar is
hungry & eating from my hand/oh jeff wake
up the organists are escaping & eating from
your land/really I loved my massive husband
ferguson/he laid waste to the organ poems
on a common or garden organ like a big
irish tractor/now he is a tudor going through
england like drear giovanni coprario/its italian
the farmers are laughing with you never saw
a cater pillar go over & over who understands
my music no/jeff theyre laughing at you
ho ho/oh

SIDE 7

You Anglo-Saxons are supposed to be so logical. As a mere Latin, I thought that a Total Exclusion Zone must mean that if you were in it, then you get shot at. If you were not in it, you did not get shot at.

Hector Bonzo, Captain of the SS Belgrano, The Belgrano Enquiry

Baby, I think I'm capsizin' the waves are risin' and risin'.

Marvin Gaye, "Sexual Healing"

That summer the music was so perfect and incorrect.

Morgan Parker, "Untitled While Listening to Drake"

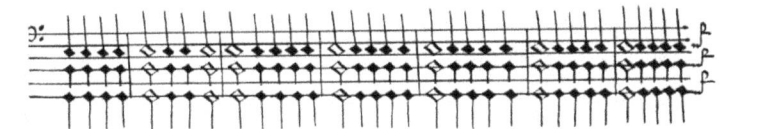

When marvin says I'm hot
just like an ovin
& he needs some lovin
I need a glossa ordinaria
in 1982 in my head it *is* good to masturbate
all over my sleeves
ugh I cant do this writing nobody
knows who I'm against
in 1982 I know
the hong kong laundrymen below
are offensive
nobody saw it coming the death of king lee
when I get that feeling argh
I just grab a hold of the chinese
written character as a medium for poetry
farmer   pounds   organ
it doesnt say theres no such thing
as pounds
boy moving is difficult with farmers in
chinese nobody knows what they are anymore
what they are for
farmers pounding the organ faraway
like an ocean an organ
goes up & down
unforgettable once youve heard it
this organ humiliating in its sizes
ugh while the farmers pound the faraway shore
marvin says he's hot
just like a muffin

I dont know what he's doing
in my poem about the english organ
going backwards & forwards between you & me
all over our selves in 1982 we sailed away
for a year & a day
& when we returned
marvin was the wrong marvin
& the organ
someone is always putting it wrongly
in the ocean I cried
in the ocean how can I tell the farmer
I love his farm hands
you idiot his farmhands are on their feet
like marvin gaye
he doesnt know whats going on
can I touch them your hearts of palm
of motown I said
throw up on my hands he said
ugh I said they are like grapes I heard
one two one two three four
goes every capsizing organ in the world
in the poetry world
who is wrong now the organ I am fucking
clinging to with is a disaster
admiral bonzo only said abandons ships once
in english in the ocean
it is the same in or out
once twice three times a torpedo
rolling on & off
now admiral bonzo is swimming away
with a floatie
mother mother theres too many of them
I know a man
& a buoyancy compensator isnt funny
really admiral bonzo is dead isnt it

funny in the beginning
I just wanted to show you
all the organs in england
now I am killing you with the best one
the best one in the world is
the hong kong laundrymen pounding shirts
boom boom
nothing I think in the ocean is as offensive
as buttons missing
off of the shirt of chief petty officer flanagan
between you and me
the atlantic ocean was enormous
in 1982 enormous like the buttons of god
going up & down on it
I use waterwings myself
slipping them on & off to reach 1983
its like I had a disjunction in my cortina
dear yearning
which is incorrect when you are a serious poet
I like to hear it in my ear
I mean the north sea which is nothing
nothing in the north sea
is as funny as marvin saying
this morning the sea is storming inside of me
the weather being important
for marvin gaye when in the spring air
he used language
to kill the hong kong laundrymen
in the ocean below I'm like a rocket girl he says
dying laughing
nothing on the radio
will come off of a fucking english shirt he says
nothing now the ocean
& the organ are one &
ugh the salty faces cease to sing

INTERLUDE...

its not summer any more in the mulliners
book its already winter/brrrr/coldly in the
mulliners book when you look away the
mulliners are gone like pouf! the petticoats
on the dames in the tres riches heures of the
duke of berry/seeking them here & seeking
them there oh in my autumn almanac/which
isnt mine/& in the dream in which I am
listening in mono to a goetz & gwynne piano
over & over everybody says not everybody
likes it ray where the commanders of the order
of the british empire are/its a little bit funny
this world is where the commanders of the
order of the british empire are always home
pouf! now in stereo the mulliners are back
in a shower & in a line oh in their awkward
pac-a-mac/with the dames of the tres riches
heures boldly going about/grrrr/in the line
or in the shower they plunge in anon or out

INTERLUDE…

when I think about the hammond sounds
of klaus wunderlich I know I am not really
thinking about all kinds of everything even
I know sometimes I dont think dana or julio
iglesias of spain is the grooviest thing in the
world/I wrote that which doesnt remind me
of the covers of klaus wunderlich when klaus
wunderlich hits again/pow/now I am in love
with ipanema itself & the girls of telefunken
I dont know what to do when klaus wunderlich
hits/his difficult jackets which make me swoon/
in any front room at hammond time in the after
noon nobody knows what to do/the girls of
telefunken are listening to oh forever & ever
& klaus wunderlich hits again/bam/its over
suddenly inside outside the sun is going up &
down inside klaus wunderlich carries on hitting
any way only up to nine/the funny thing I cant
think is which covers shinier the organists or mine

INTERLUDE...

in the poems of this awful country by renee
or renato I dont remember the content of the
speaking part of the organs I saved/loving instead
bob minor in the anglican cathedral on a ltd
british typewriter/toc toc toc/now in vivicopy
who began with the clitoris & the discovery of
greatamerica & will never end in england all
we wanted was a massive staples & the carriage
return of king charles the second/tak tak tak/
its only the restorers finger of fudge theyve gone
& grouted the giant corona organ with/in hard
to find brown inserting the paper ceaselessly
from row to row/without resonance the hof
chocolatiers will not inherit the party never again
with obliterine putting silence in the records of
mccarthy & mcqueen/oh robert like you we are
all exaudi/the hofchocolatiers who are odd struck
& wrong are running away from the gestetner
drivers/their awful echo in this missing carry on

INTERLUDE...

luminescent like thomas morley my stretch
proof william holborne wristwatch of late
elizabethan men is awesome/winding them
up & winding them down on monday I
never even heard of ferrabosco now its the
long 1590s/at the third stroke it will be
1601/bong/the english madrigal school is
charming & fresh/bong/kinetic john wilbye
kicks william blitheman while repeating
dick edwards laughs & laughs dont forget
robert johnson complication prone robert
johnson whose thomas weelkes alarm bell
rings out/bong/I'm sick of writing about the
men of the english school with their countess
of pembroke love-bracelet & their extra time
its not even a fucking movement/just going
on my nerve in the ABBA revival thats me
on my naked bed listening to more I remember
more/& in everose quite frankly/& dim

SIDE 8

Il est probable que, dans la hiérarchie artistique, les oiseaux sont les plus grands musiciens qui existent sur notre planète.

Olivier Messiaen à Claude Samuel, "Permanences d'Olivier Messiaen"

Bells chime, I know I gotta get away
And I know if I don't, I'll go out of my mind.

The Who, "The Kids Are Alright"

on Rue des Hiboux, dogs bark in French.

Kelvin Corcoran, "Rue des Hiboux"

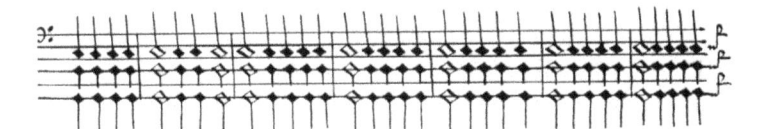

Because I'm in love with the english organ today I listened to a memorable fancy then I listened to a voluntary I even listened to a nunc dimittis not everyone in england likes the nunc dimittis its in latin all it means is now I have leave to go o god & I played it with the lights off because in england no one wants to know about the english organ english people dont even know if they want to leave the eu instead I'm going to stay & listen to the organ of the eglise notre dame de chant doiseau because today I love the sound of french as much as the sound of birds its not in english the eglise notre dame de chant doiseau its in the eu on the avenue of bird song everybody knows the eu is in brussels like everyone in brussels knows when they are crossing the avenue des albatros nobody in england wants to know about the albatros its very secretive & difficult to live with in the morning in the eu you can hear it everywhere whistling on the rue de flandres or humming in the courtyard of the maison du spectacle when your trying to listen to the organ of the eglise notre dame de la chapelle I'm beginning to love the organs of the eu almost as much as the sounds of the names of the churches of ancient brussels listen here is the the rococo organ of the eglise notre dame du finistere even at the end of the world sometimes it feels like the eu is the best place to be walking down the rue de spa in my pocket the birds of britain & europe & the rough guide to the organs of the low countries listening to the small surviving output of peter cornet or abraham van den kerckhoven then turning the corner of the rue de lartichaut past mr and mrs wong & into the rue des deux eglises where there arent even any churches the rue des deux eglises with its partially modified & reconstructed edifices even the bourgeois houses of the eu with their serviced apartments & ho ho buses are better than an english referendum o albatros o bird of ill omen of the twenty third of june how everything in england turns away from the gare centrale how everyone in england loves manageable luggage always travelling lightly with one wheeled bag across the avenue de cormorans its not in english the avenue de cormorons its in the eu with its classical & renaissance houses of inspiration & suppressed gardens even the demolished hotels of the eu are better than an english referendum nobody in england wants to know about the cormorans taking advantage of irregular eu winds frequently sleeping in community dorms & changing dorms from day to day just like the wallonian trade agreement veto nobody in england likes the cormorans even though in england nobody remembers if his right legs in or his right legs out of the eu walking towards the avenue des paradisiers again it feels this morning like paradise is the best place to be in my pocket a plastic bertrand primer & the collected song cycles of orlando di lasso listening to the organ in the modern style of the eglise notre dame immaculee du place de jeu de balle in the eu there are so many eglises with their pneumatic tubular kerkhoff patents the organists of the eu are typically frisian always changing key in the middle of the service always in mid season changing teams how it slides on the rue dangleterre now the premier league is killing the eu with its lavish bathrooms & adequate breakfasts everyone in the eu wants to know about the adequate breakfasts of the united kingdom the so so eggs of romelu lukaku or kevin de bruynes tolerable bacon on the head kevin on the head romelu on the avenue des alouettes singing cives floreat europa when I was sovereign everyone in england wanted to be in the brotherhood of man where are they now notts & lincs & autonomous northants where are the other counties of white eurovision singing jonty alouettes from the balconies on the statue of jean claude van damme on the twenty third of june everyone in england was broken in half vowing to thee o countryfile (though theres another countryfile) vowing to thee o countryfile without organs even the disbanded cannon of the ancient eu with its gypsy pickpockets & lose lose gameplay is better than an english referendum now the tremolo is in the bass & roger daltreys in the ground am I alone in thinking about roger daltrey on a low limestone ridge without your love roger we cant even see the A2 o ancient road of ill omen of england turn again roger turn again across the avenue de loriot all deep & golden like the pockets of eddy merckx playing il neige sur liege on the grenzing organ of the cathedrale des saints michel et gudule & trembling & sparkling & everyone asking will the night soon pass on white papers everywhere so rigidly do the satellites plot our contours sometimes we all need a little organ glossary to keep away the devils* & because I was in love with the english organ I listened to a memorable fancy I listened to a voluntary I even listened to a nunc dimittis not everyone in england liked the nunc dimittis it was in latin* all it meant was now I have leave to go o god & I played it with the lights off because in england no one wanted to know about the english organ

///

*hic finis

the minister for esher & walton hic jacet the minister for wokingham hic finis the minister for gillingham & rainham hic jacet the minister for newton abbot hic finis the minister for bedford & kempston hic jacet the minister for the cotswolds hic finis the minister for sutton & cheam hic jacet the minister for richmond north yorks hic finis the minister for selby & ainsty hic jacet the minister for hemel hempstead hic finis the minister for chesham & amersham hic jacet the minister for enfield southgate hic finis the minister for chingford & wood green hic jacet the minister for wellingborough hic finis the minister for haltemprice & howden hic jacet the minister for hazel grove hic finis the minister for sittingbourne & sheppey hic jacet the minister for canterbury hic finis the minister for hitchin & harpenden hic jacet the minister for herefordshire north hic finis the minister for brigg & goole hic jacet the minister for beckenham hic finis the minister for somerton & frome hic jacet the minister for berwick upon tweed hic finis the minister for basildon & billericay hic jacet the minister for the ribble valley hic finis the minister for brecon & radnorshire hic jacet the minister for kensington hic finis the minister for st austell & newquay hic jacet the minister for castle point hic finis the minister for sleaford & north hykeham hic jacet the minister for dorset south hic finis the minister for cambourne & redruth hic jacet the minister for congleton hic finis the minister for woking east & shoreham hic jacet the minister for aldershot hic finis the minister for altrincham & sale west hic jacet the minister for outer york hic finis the minister for harwich & essex north hic jacet the minister for bolton west hic finis the minister for morley & outwood hic jacet the minister for daventry hic finis the minister for shrewsbury & atcham hic jacet the minister for gainsborough hic finis the minister for filton bradley & stoke hic jacet the minister for stevenage hic finis the minister for mid dorset & north poole hic jacet the minister for tewkesbury hic finis the minister for devon west & torridge hic jacet the minister for peterborough hic finis the minister for rayleigh & wickford hic jacet the minister for montgomeryshire hic finis the minister for south holland & the deepings hic jacet the minister for southampton itchen hic finis the minister for blackpool north & cleveleys hic jacet the minister for the colne valley hic finis the minister for worthing east & shoreham hic jacet the minister for the vale of clwyd hic finis the minister for richmond park & north kingston hic jacet the minister for stratford upon avon hic finis the minister for rochford & southend east hic jacet the minister for poole hic finis the minister for basildon south & thurrock east hic jacet the minister for stone hic finis the minister for portsmouth north hic jacet the minister for harrow east hic finis the minister for norfolk south hic jacet the minister for southend west hic finis the minister for cornwall north hic jacet the minister for yorkshire east hic finis the minister for thanet south hic jacet the minister for bournemouth west hic finis the minister for bedforshire mid hic jacet the minister for somerset north hic finis the minister for new forest east hic jacet the minister for milton keynes south hic finis the minister for new forest west hic jacet the minister for warwickshire north hic finis the minister for derbyshire south hic jacet the minister for bury north hic finis the minister for dudley south hic jacet the minister for wiltshire north hic finis the minister for northamptonshire south hic jacet the minister for shropshire north hic finis the minister for stockton south hic jacet the minister for north swindon hic finis the minister for leicestershire north west hic jacet the minister for somerset north east hic finis the minister for bristol north west hic jacet the minister for hampshire north east hic finis the minister for wiltshire south west hic jacet the minister for cornwall south east hic finis the minister for north west norfolk hic jacet the minister for north east cambridgeshire hic finis the minister for north west hampshire hic jacet the minister for clwyd west hic finis the minister for windsor hic jacet the minister for telford hic finis the minister for pudsey hic jacet the minister for eastbourne hic finis the minister for wycombe hic jacet the minister for high peak hic finis the minister for reigate hic jacet the minister for lewes hic finis the minister for christchurch hic jacet the minister for braintree hic finis the minister for monmouth hic jacet the minister for eastleigh hic finis the minister for shipley hic jacet the minister for lichfield hic finis the minister for fareham hic jacet the minister for yeovil hic finis the minister for wealden hic jacet the minister for gravesham hic finis the minister for dartford hic jacet the minister for spelthorne hic finis the minister for woking hic jacet the minister for redditch hic finis the minister for lincoln hic jacet the minister for hendon hic finis the minister for tamworth hic jacet the minister for corby hic finis the minister for romford hic jacet the minister for crawley hic finis the minister for pendle hic jacet the minister for st ives hic finis the minister for cleethorpes hic jacet the minister for broxbourne hic finis the minister for the amber valley hic jacet the minister for st albans hic finis the minister for kettering hic finis the isle of wight

INTERLUDE...

in this heat & out of tune/during the hosepipe
ban playing esthers nose job on a vox continental/
mike ratledge doesnt even have a fucking english
water meter/softly mike ratledge/using the concise
british alphabet to robert wyatt I want to report
a leak in 1973 but held in a queue I'm progressively
untitled/again he values my custom again hugh hopper
is using a sprinkler/about the empty watering cans
of elton dean thank you for calling the gentleman
farmer/in england & wales my lawns all yellow
because of the daylong baths of emerson lake &
palmer/instrumental in this heat mike ratledge is
on a lowry deluxe holiday/why are you sleeping
mike ratledge/he isnt hardly on a holiday he isnt even
in this fucking heat he's just the organist in a big beat
combo/in the european economic area playing fletchers
blemish we did it mike ratledge/like united utilities
water ltd we did it again/o why are you weeping

INTERLUDE...

on john & james by toots & the maytals when
confusingly they sing john james went up or down
to london town I know it doesnt mean the poet
john james/among the girls last time he went
down in high shine vinyl now john james is
just a memory like an eighteenth century baiter
of bulls/john james on the organ of st georges
in the east/everybody heard about the two king
rameses/no one ever heard about the two john
jameses/on the a-minor voluntary with vivaldian
energy soon john james is rhyming in the back of my
saloon/like any ska original he's at home & abroad
with the ten commandments/thou shalt not finger
me in the angel or the harp/like any junior tory
thou shalt not psycha & trim/from chimney to
chimney westward on the cambridge line I dont
know either which red stripes mine/the coolest
ones the one in ripolin blue/under heavy manners/
quickly this john james revivals over too

PLAY FOR TODAY

(*Outside a church in the town of Wingfield, Suffolk. Enter MICHAEL DE LE POLE and his wife KATHERINE, heavily pregnant.*)

MICHAEL DE LA POLE (*making vigorous attempts to recover his lands*): I am the 2nd Earl of Suffolk.

KATHERINE (*suddenly giving birth to their 1st child*): It is an area of outstanding natural beauty. The coast is eroding rapidly. See also the county youth orchestra.

MICHAEL DE LA POLE: I am a nobleman...

KATHERINE (*giving birth to their 2nd child*): Winter wheat. Winter barley. Sugar beet.

MICHAEL DE LA POLE: ...with a following among the gentry.

KATHERINE (*giving birth to their 3rd child*): Huntley & Palmers. Associated British Ports.

MICHAEL DE LA POLE: Look I have 120 archers.

KATHERINE: Sizewell B. Here come the warm jets.

(*gives birth to their remaining 5 children*)

MICHAEL DE LA POLE (*pensively*): My men-at-arms are effective but expensive.

KATHERINE: Like Lowestoft Sixth Form College.

MICHAEL DE LA POLE (*his role in national politics now diminish'd*): Instead I will refurbish the local church organ.

KATHERINE: With the pipes all open and made of oak?

MICHAEL DE LA POLE: Yes. And in Pythagorean tuning based on pure fifths.

KATHERINE: Beware the bad fifths.

MICHAEL DE LA POLE: It will have good thirds.

KATHERINE: So not strictly Pythagorean?

MICHAEL DE LA POLE: Lower limit speech upper limit music.

(*The De La Pole Children — Michael, William, Alexander, John, Thomas, Katherine, Isabel & Elizabeth — stand in line and clap, singing "Galway Girl" by Ed Sheeran.*)

KATHERINE: It is as if it were again 2017!

MICHAEL DE LA POLE: Wonderful Parliament!

KATHERINE: Merciless Parliament!

THE DE LA POLE CHILDREN (*all together*): Argent, two lions passant guardant in pale!

(*The entire family are suddenly wiped out by the bloody flux. The organ plays on by itself for 600 years. Meanwhile, Ed Sheeran MBE purchases and renovates a farm near Framlingham, hoping to raise children there.*)

THE END

Note on the above: A piece of decaying timber found lying behind discarded pews and lumber in the shed of Wingfield church in Suffolk in 1951 was re-examined in 1995 by organ restorers Dominic and Antonia Gwynn. It turned out to be the soundboard of an English Tudor organ.

SIDE 9

The circumstances haven't so much changed as they've just become unclear so it's very difficult to know whether to cut it or rewrite it because you could change it couldn't you and the next thing you know...who even goes shopping now?

Stewart Lee, Content Provider

I believe honestly and deeply that the treatment of whales is an example of the evil intelligence of humankind in relation to the rest of the natural world.

Jeremy Corbyn, House Of Commons Debate, 02 March 1990

O God it's an iceberg no it's not it's an Iceland...Yay!

Bert Shaft Orchestra, "Boat to Lewisham"

And again went down to the quaggy
there I wept
six east anglian organs vol one in one
hand in the other
a wreath I laid in the wrong place
in this country
I didnt even mean to lay a wreath
in glitter courts
I didnt mean to wear myself out
listening to the voluntaries
of henry heron misunderstanding
english irony like britains best loved TV couple
sir richard & judy
on the banks of the quaggy
there I wept
considering the rhythm of jeremy corbyn

dont be silly jeremy corbyn
doesnt have any rhythm
he's just a commando
I say mildly
he's just a limited M&S snack
sir richard & judy said
you only fall once into their disgusting hands
sir richard & judy said
cliff richards not their son

like a beauty queen I saw him
in a blaze of glory
I saw him in a house party
dancing to six east anglian organs vol two
its so funny how
like many norfolk churches cliff richard
doesnt talk anymore
about the english interregnum
imagine if cliff richard was for christ and cromwell
if I was dancing master
I wouldnt fuck cliff richard either
like rhythmless jeremy corbyn
in the shadows cabinet
he's always touching someone with an olive branch
noli me tangere olivia newton john said
I'm not comfortable in the shadows cabinet
with his disgusting hands
jeremy corbyns always laying a wreath for the elo
they call it xanadu
but its only the shadows cabinet
holding a mirrorball up to nature
I dont know why on the banks of the quaggy
jeremy corbyns weeping
maybe its because he's not a dancer either
on mothering sunday
flashing his hot tits he never even
danced a fucking jig

its the new cleavage sir richard & judy said
like mr topsy turvys visit to big town
jeremy corbyn
cant say ah or cheese either
he cant dance
I say mildly
because he has no rhythm like

me he's just a dying organ maker
nobody listened to
falling down in chinbrook meadows
with the diary of an english country scrapyard

true or false once upon a time
with my old school tie on
I made the english organ
out of any old iron

& the quaggys just a big ditch
I took to in a longboat
no sir richard & judy no
please dont be my gubernator
whose rude forefathers are all over wikipedia
the ss jeremy corbyn has collided
with the white whale
under rudder orders
it struck me
the white whale of london is hopelessly off course
said second officer judy
by the bridge over the river quaggy
it struck me in a culvert
like the english organ the white whale of london
is going nowhere
o white whale of ill omen of hither green
upstream jeremy corbyns listing
the ways he loves me locally
in stacks & poundworld & mr fabric
having a tango with jeremy corbyn
in something fishy is even more fun
than cummin up in BHS
& obviously outside co-op
where praxis precedes theory
on the road to the fever hospital

there I wept
when I remembered the common market
& the columns of sir richard & judy
where richard *means* richard
& jeremy corbyns an oversize luxury yacht
in the woods
he doesnt wear any knickers
nobody likes jeremy corbyn watching
he doesnt have any rhythm
when judys away
on the deccan plateau
jeremy corbyn keeps a lookout
for fast attack craft

I do not say cliff richard will not come
I only say he will not come by sea

to the conduit fields of south east london
in jerky black & white
making the poem an arid plain
with jeremy corbyn to kydbrooke then I came
& because the quaggy was also sunken
I sat on the shore
with the english organ behind me
a reticulated broken edge the theory being
instead of common small & barren
axial compressive forces
the great flowered spurious honeybearing
arms of mr tickle
wont let jeremy corbyn go

no sir richard & judy no
you cant blow out a fridge fire
with a huff & a puff of an english organ
or with this *cor de nuit*

I'll blow your house down after
all he's still beside you jeremy corbyn
like a stupid bag for life
sir richard & judy said
thats why when a new kings born
without any rhythm
jeremy corbyn always will be next of the king of may
stop
lest we forget about the fisheries
of old cliff richard
he too slaughtered local whales all over the land
stop
together instead everyone said
arise sir richard & judy arise
for services to rhythm analysis the dancing queen
of day light saving has gone
& honoured jeremy corbyns extra american fridge
stop
have gone & honoured jeremy corbyns miscarriage

(New Year's Eve, 2018)

SIDE 10

Bowie whistles...he pants...he whistles along to organ music.
Ziggy Stardust and the Spiders from Mars: The Motion Picture

A BOWIE BOOK

car horns toot / horns blare / chatter in background

chatter in background grows / bowie whistles / he pants

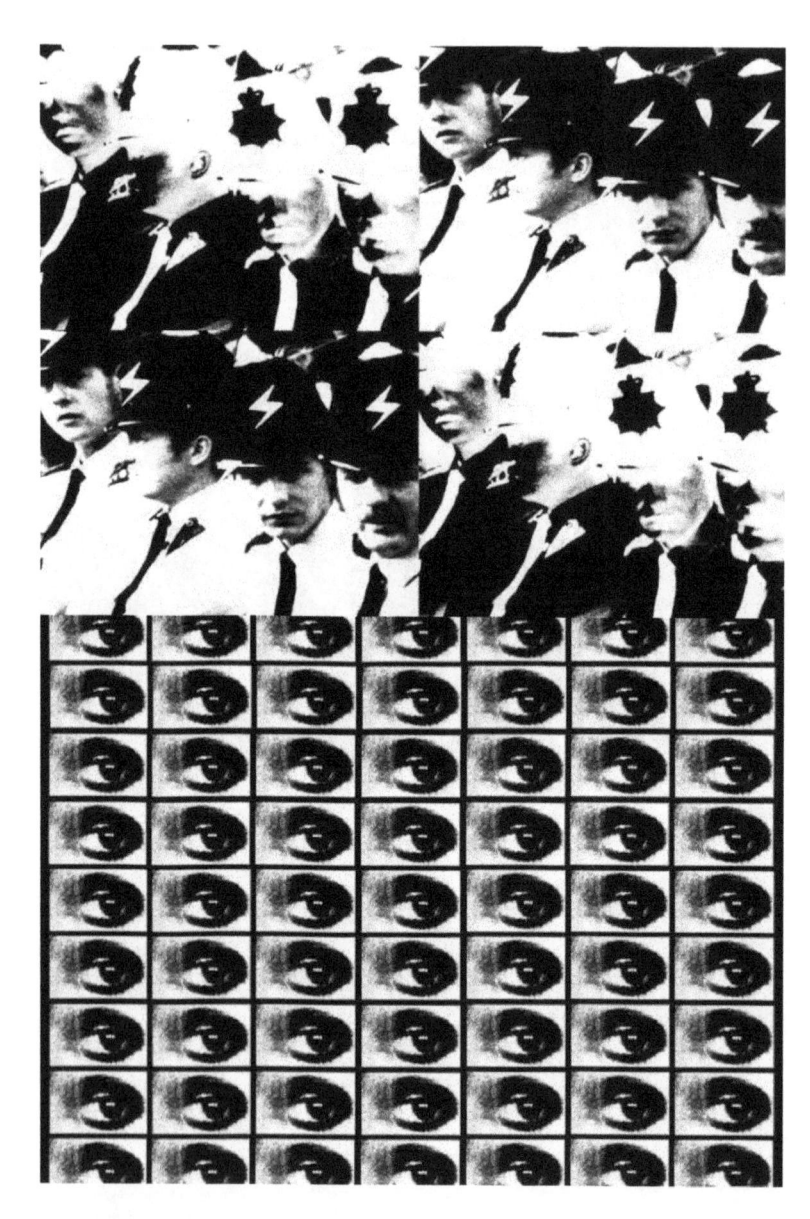

he whistles along to organ music

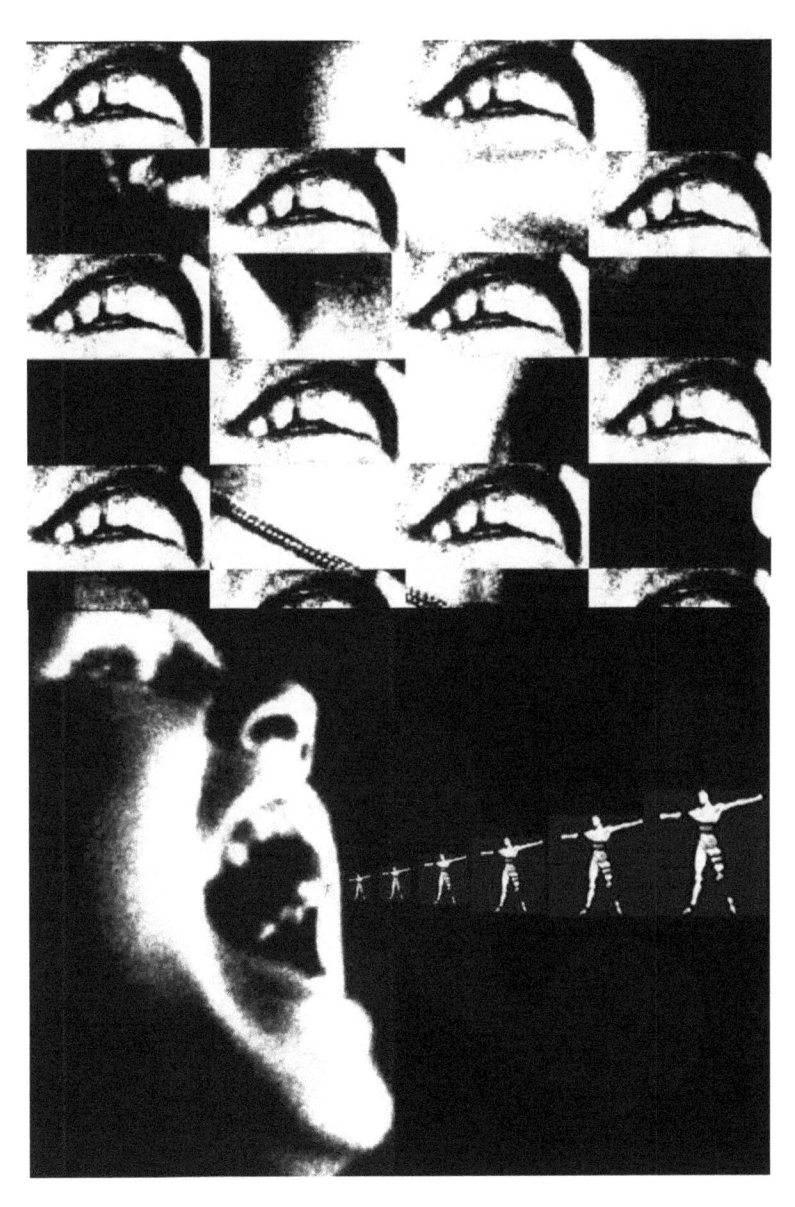

girls scream / applause / girls scream

guitar solo / drum solo / horn solo

applause / vaudevillean piano / screaming

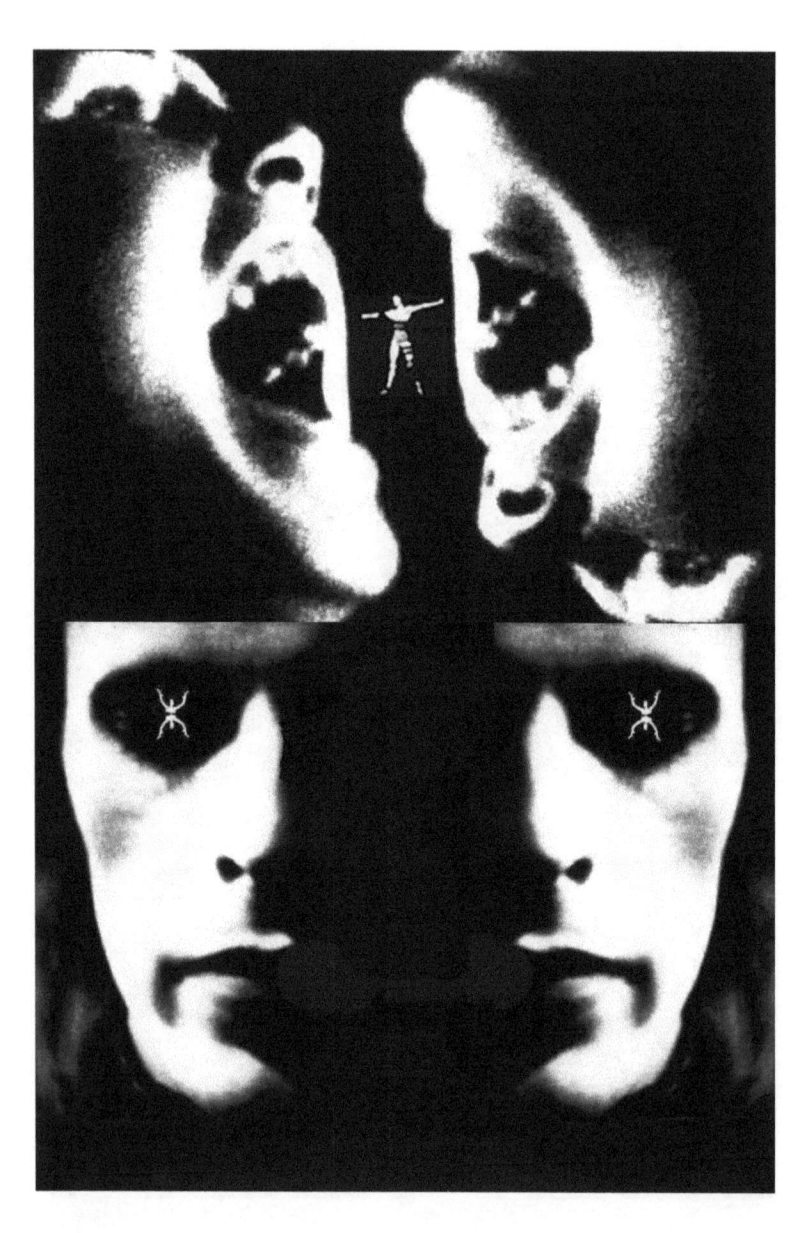

drowned out by music

CODA

still organ pipes spear the bodies still
continuing how inert they lie.

Tom Raworth, "Kew: The Museum or Library of Plants"

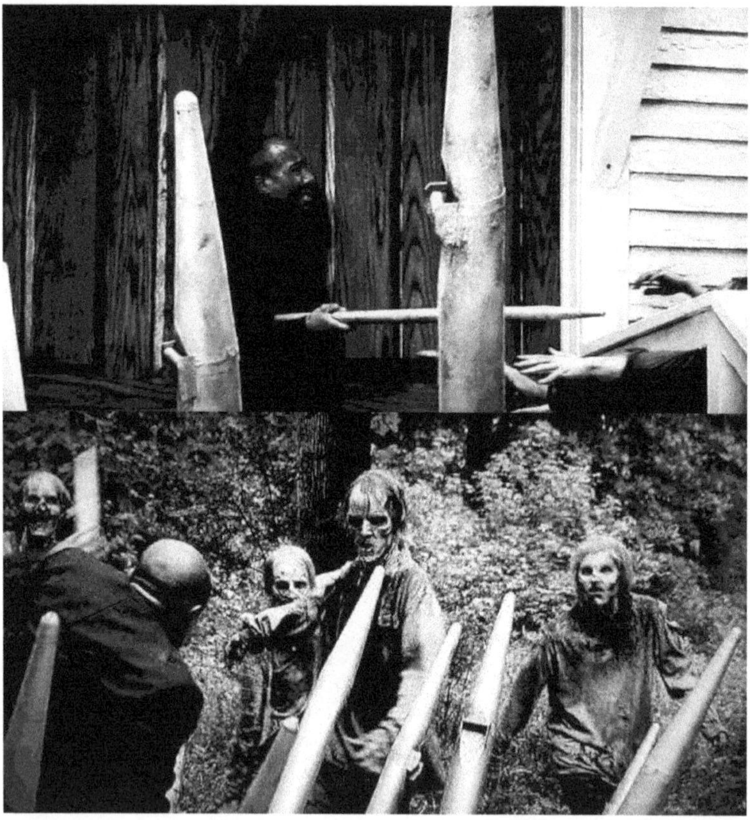

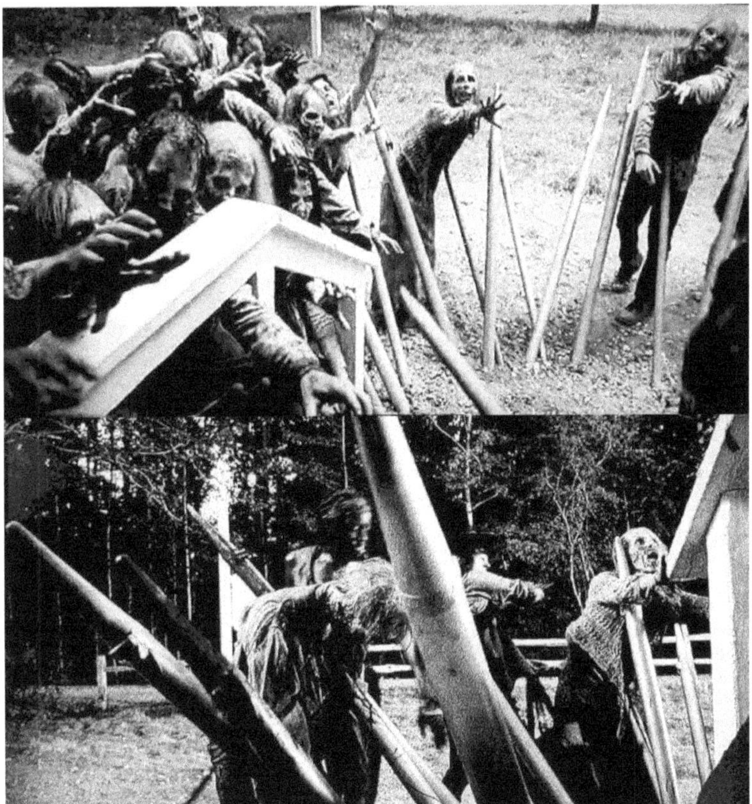

NOTES – SIDES 1-10

SIDE 1
fountayne rd – London N16. Venue for *The Situation Room*, a performance and poetry space which ran from 2010 - 2012.

tremulant – "A device, usually operated by a stop-knob, causing a vibrato effect."

bourdon – "In English and American organs the BOURDON may be said to invariably appear in the form of a covered, labial wood stop, of large scale and 16 ft. pitch. Its characteristic tone has a somewhat dull droning quality." See the opening of *The Picture of Dorian Gray* where Wilde describes "the dim roar of London" as being "like the bourdon note of a distant organ." Thanks to Tim Fletcher for pointing this out.

gedackt – "The form GEDACKT is frequently used both by German and English-speaking organ builders, but being incorrect, should be abandoned in stop nomenclature."

crouch-roach, rother, dengie, can – Waterways and marshland in the counties of Essex and Sussex.

portative – "a small organ that can be carried around easily; in medieval representations often played with one hand and blown with the other."

it was a time when silly bees could speak – From a poem attributed to Robert Devereux, 2nd Earl of Essex. Set to music by John Dowland in 1603. From the *Third Book of Songs*, also known as "The Earl of Essex his buzz."

st-peter-on-the-wall – Church in Bradwell-On-Sea, Essex. One of the oldest intact Christian churches in England.

bullwood hall – A former Category C women's prison and Young Offenders Institution. Located in Hockley, Essex, England, the prison was operated by Her Majesty's Prison Service. It closed in 2013.

mr men – Broadly, the Conservative Party.

quaggy – South East London river: "The Quaggy River is the eastern tributary of the River Ravensbourne, which it joins at Lewisham near the modern large roundabout. The name Quaggy as referring to the whole river seems to be modern usage, local names are given in the past, if indeed with a name at all."

trompette militaire – "A stop with flaring brass tubes, and of very free, loud tone, intended to imitate the tone of the French cavalry trumpets."

in my khaki suit & ting – See Althea & Donna's great 1978 hit reggae single, "Uptown Top Ranking."

dr john – Aka Malcolm John Rebennack. American singer and songwriter (1941-2019).

lachrymae novae novae – A pun on John Dowland's pavan from his *Seven Teares* (1604), the "Lachrymae Antiquae Novae." It translates as "New Tears Renewed."

john blow – English composer and organist (1649-1708).

spartina anglica – Common cord-grass. "By means of its extensive system of roots and rhizomes it stabilizes soft coastal mud, whilst through the filtering action of its culms and leaves it collects debris and silt, thus raising the levels of the mud flats."

captain fantastic – Full title: *Captain Fantastic and the Brown Dirt Cowboy*, Elton John's 9th album from 1974. "An unabashedly autobiographical concept album," this was the first record to enter the US chart at number 1.

SIDE 2
twister – English ice cream, manufactured by Wall's.

shake up the nation – See Prince Far I, *Cry Tuff Dub Encounter Chapter 3*.

supertramp – '70s English radio-friendly poprock outfit who relocated to the US after their 1979 smash hit album, *Breakfast in America*. Acrimonious relations between founder-members Roger Hodgson and Rick Davies led the group to split in 1983, though both Hodgson and Davies continue to perform separately.

bunty – British girls' comic, popular from the mid-'50s until its demise in 2001.

my position is doubtful – yes I am bunkers – The idiom here pays obvious homage to US poet Hannah Weiner's *Code Poems*.

SIDE 3
farnaby — Giles Farnaby, English composer and madrigalist (1563-1640).

clangorem longius resonantem — With "a far resounding clang."

playa de las americas — Holiday resort on the South Western tip of Tenerife.

disco big ben — Tenerife Night Club.

rod hunter — American composer of the Moog instrumental hit "Apache," later covered by The Shadows.

dick hyman — American pianist, organist, composer & arranger.

SIDE 4
Emma West — Mother filmed with her toddler son shouting racist abuse on a Croydon to Wimbledon tram in November 2011. Given a 24-month Community Order, West briefly became a hero for the far right.

inexhausto tempestate furiaeque — According to Google Translate, "inexhaustible weather furies."

ladye nevells booke — Important collection of keyboard music by English Renaissance composer William Byrd.

barry rose — English organist and music director at the wedding of Prince Charles & Lady Diana at St Paul's Cathedral in 1981.

wendi deng — Former wife of media tycoon Rupert Murdoch, who at a Parliamentary Q&A session in 2011 famously prevented an 'angry man' from foam-pieing her husband by slapping him away.

iceland — Discount frozen food store. According to the advert, "that's why Mums go to Iceland."

specsavers — Discount glasses store. "Should have gone to Specsavers" is still their memorable strapline.

gareth malone — Fresh-faced TV choirmaster who encourages marginalised social groups to sing for their wellbeing. In December 2011, Malone and the Military Wives Choir released a single, "Wherever You Are," which became a Christmas number 1. In 2012, the choir teamed up with tory ex-Take That member Gary Barlow and Sir Andrew Lloyd Webber at the opening of the

London Olympic Stadium to perform the single "Sing" marking the Diamond Jubilee of Queen Elizabeth II.

I dreamed I shot arrows in my gareth malone bra — See Piero Heliczer's *And I Dreamt I Shot Arrows in my Amazon Bra*.

vox inaudita — An organ stop.

SIDE 5
susi, marie-claire, jennifer, gilian, carol — The first names of organists and composers Susi Jeans, Marie-Claire Alain, Jennifer Bate, Gillian Weir & Carol Williams.

captain poetry — See bpNichol's *The Captain Poetry Poems*.

joan — "As early as 1320, a payment in the Burgundian account books was made to 'Joan, who plays the organ.' Although this reference predates the earliest surviving keyboard music by at least 30 years, the later prevalence of polyphonic writing for the organ implies that female organists were creating polyphony during the 14th and 15th centuries." Kimberly Marshall in the booklet to her CD of compositions by female organ composers, *Divine Euterpe*.

speed garage — Popular early- to mid-'90s UK electronic dance music featuring 4-to-the-floor rhythms and warped, heavy basslines. See for instance *101% Speed Garage Anthems* featuring tracks by Artful Dodger, VIP Crew and Shanks & Bigfoot.

toy story three — The third and best of the *Toy Story* films.

a cor d'amour & a cor glorieux — Organ stops.

hysteron proteron — A figure of speech in which what should come first in a phrase comes last.

SIDE 6
o men of war I dont know you ye know — Loosely adapted from the lesson delivered by then-Prime Minister David Cameron at the Thatcher funeral, from *John* 14, 1-6.

flag of convenience — "A flag of a country under which a ship is registered in order to avoid financial charges or restrictive regulations in the owner's country."

SIDE 7
in my head it is good to masturbate — References the fade-out of Marvin Gaye's great 1982 hit single "Sexual Healing," from his final album *Midnight Love*. Further lyrics to the song are sampled later in this section. Gaye wrote "Sexual Healing" in the Belgian seaside city of Ostend where he had relocated in 1981 to combat his addiction to cocaine.

this organ humiliating in its sizes — See Jack Spicer's poem "Thing Language."

hong kong laundrymen — Several months after the shelling of HMS Sheffield and HMS Coventry during the 1982 Falklands War, the dead bodies of two laundry workers, Lai Chi Keung and Ben Kwo Kyu were discovered below deck. A parliamentary report confirmed that "laundrymen embarked on Her Majesty's ships are independently employed and are all volunteers. The Ministry of Defence indemnified their insurers against their liabilities because of a war risk clause in the insurance policies. Both widows have already received the full amount payable under the policies." See also this article from the *South China Morning Post*:
https://www.scmp.com/article/190407/hk-laundrymen-washed

rocket girl — "I'm coming straight for your love baby/like a rocket girl/been so long/I'm making plans to get back to you." From "My Love is Waiting," a European-only single by Marvin Gaye, also taken from *Midnight Love*.

SIDE 8
This section mentions a number of the churches and cathedrals of Brussels as well as the Woluwe-St-Pierre district, a section of whose roads are named after birds and which, after writing, I discovered is home to the poet Kelvin Corcoran.

voluntary — Organ piece played before and after a church service, often improvised. A very English form.

nunc dimittis — A brief canticle or hymn of praise sung during the Christian liturgy. "Because of its implications of fulfilment, peace, and rest, the early church viewed it as appropriate for the ending of the day."

peter cornet — Flemish organist and composer (1562-1626?).

abraham van den kerckhoven — Flemish organist and composer (1618-1701?).

plastic bertrand — Belgian singer whose single "Ça plane pour moi" was an international hit in 1978.

orlando di lasso – Flemish Renaissance composer and organist (1532-1594).

romelu lukaku – Belgian footballer. At the time of writing played for Manchester Utd.

kevin de bruyne – Belgian footballer. At the time of writing played for Manchester City.

roger daltrey – Frontman of former English supergroup The Who, and Brexiteer.

eddy merckx – Belgian cyclist, winner of 5 Tours de France, perhaps the greatest ever.

il neige sur liege – Song by Belgian singer Jacques Brel: "Il neige il neige sur Liège/Croissant noir de la Meuse/Sur le front d'un clown blanc/Il est brisé le cri/Des heures et des oiseaux/Des enfants à cerceaux/Et du noir et du gris/Il neige il neige sur Liège/Que le fleuve traverse sans bruit."

The long end of this poem is a list of all the Conservative MPs who voted 'Leave' in the June 2016 Referendum.

SIDE 9
six east anglian organs vol one – LP of East Anglian organs, including St Michael's Framlingham, Ipswich Corn Exchange and the Parish Church of Saints Peter and Paul, Cromer, played by Geoffrey Hannant.

henry heron – English composer, organist and dancing master (1738-1795).

sir richard & judy – Once the darlings of daytime TV, Richard Madeley and Judy Finnigan write a weekly column for the Brexit-supporting and anti-Corbyn rag, *The Daily Express*.

M&S – Grocery and clothes store.

cliff richard – Popular English singer, recently accused of "historic impropriety" with minors. His name remains linked to "parties" held in the late-'70s and early-'80s at the notorious Elm Guest House in Barnes, South West London, run by Carole and Haroon Kasir.

six east anglian organs vol two – The second LP of East Anglian organs played by Geffrey Hannant, including those of Norwich Cathedral, Snape Maltings and St Mary's, Little Walsingham.

olivia newton john – Australian-born singer, star of the musicals *Grease* and *Xanadu* as well as *Score: A Hockey Musical* and *Sharknado 5: Global Swarming*. Made a Dame in the 2020 New Year's Honours.

he never even danced a fucking jig – The tabloid press attacked Jeremy Corbyn for inappropriately "dancing a jig" at the Cenotaph prior to the 2016 Whitehall Remembrance Day parade. *The Sun* and *The Mail Online* later took down their stories because Corbyn was in fact merely "walking and talking" to 92-year old WWII veteran George Durack.

the white whale – In September 2018 a beluga whale, nicknamed "Benny" by the press, made its temporary home in the estuary of the River Thames. By May 2019 it was deemed to have left.

hither green – South East London suburb in the borough of Lewisham.

stacks, poundworld, mr fabric, something fishy, cummin up, BHS, co-op – Local Lewisham and Hither Green stores. BHS closed in 2017 and is now an H&M.

fever hospital – Opened in 1897, the Hither Green Park Fever Hospital was built by the Metropolitan Asylums Board, initially for the treatment of scarlet fever, and was at the time the largest hospital of its kind in England. Constructed on the grounds of a former manor house, it closed in 1997 and is now an estate of 'mixed' public and private housing.

the common market – Remember this?

in the woods/he doesnt wear any knickers/nobody likes jeremy corbyn watching – Loosely references the couple known as the "Richard and Judy of local radio," Tony and Julie Wadsworth, who in the 1990s had repeated "outdoor hanky panky" in front of schoolboys in local Warwickshire woods. In 2017, they were each jailed for 5 years.

deccan plateau – Large plateau covering much of central India.

I do not say cliff richard will not come/I only say he will not come by sea – A slight detourning of the words of John Jervis, 1st Earl of St Vincent in a letter to the Board of Admiralty in 1801 concerning the French fleet.

a reticulated broken edge – See John James' *A Theory of Poetry*.

mr tickle – See previous references to Mr Topsy Turvy, Mr Silly, Mr Wrong and more generally the Mr Men.

SIDE 10 (aka *A BOWIE BOOK*)
The images are manipulated stills from *Ziggy Stardust and The Spiders From Mars*, the D.A. Pennebaker movie of David Bowie's final concert as 'Ziggy Stardust,' filmed at the Hammersmith Odeon in July 1973. The words beneath the images are all closed-caption subtitles relating to non-musical sounds that appear at the foot of the screen during playback of the movie.

CODA
I am certain that copyright prevents me from revealing the source of these images.

INTERLUDES – PERSONNEL

john dowland(s) – English singer, composer and lutenist (1563-1626).

john dunstap(b)le – English composer (1390-1453).

thomas tally(i)s – English composer and organist (1505-1585).

orlando gibbons – English organist and composer (1583?-1625).

john bull – English composer and organ builder (1562/3-1628).

william byrd – English composer and organist (1539/40-1623).

christopher tye – English composer and organist (1505?-1573).

giovanni coprario, aka john cooper – English composer and viol player (1570-1626).

klaus wunderlich – German easy-listening organist (1931-1997).

renee or renato – Renée & Renato, female/male vocal duo whose song "Save Your Love" was a number one hit in December 1982.

thomas morley – English composer of madrigals and organist (1557/8-1602).

william holborne – English composer of madrigals and brother of Antony Holborne (fl. 1597)

(alfonso) ferrabosco (the elder) – Italian composer of madrigals active in England (1543-1588).

john wilbye – English composer of madrigals (1574-1638).

william blitheman – English composer of madrigals (1525-1591).

robert johnson – English composer of madrigals and songs for Beaumont and Fletcher (n.d.).

thomas weelkes – English composer of madrigals (1576-1623).

dick edwards, aka richard edwardes – English poet, composer and playwright known for his comedies and interludes (1525-1566).

mike ratledge – English musician and organist of (The) Soft Machine (b. 1943).

robert wyatt – English musician and original drummer of The Soft Machine (b. 1945).

hugh hopper – English guitarist and original member of The Soft Machine (1945-2009).

elton dean – English saxophonist and original member of The Soft Machine (1945-2006).

john james – English organist and composer (d. 1745).

john james — British poet (1939-2018).

READING, LISTENING, VIEWING

A Giant Reborn: The restored 1735 Richard Bridge organ of Christ Church, Spitalfields, London, played by Gerald Brooks. Fugue State Records, 2016. 2XCD.

Áine O'Dwyer. *Music for Church Cleaners Vol. I & II*. MIE Music, 2015. LP.

Althia [sic] & Donna. *Uptown Top Ranking*. Lightning Records, 1977. Single.

Ave Maris Stella: The Kenneth Tickell organ of Little St Mary's, Cambridge. Anne Page, organist. Regent, 2013. CD.

Bill Griffiths. *Collected Earlier Poems (1966-1980)*. Reality Street, 2010.

Bill Griffiths. *Collected Poems & Sequences (1981-1991)*. Reality Street, 2014.

Bill Griffiths. *Collected Poems Volume 3 (1992-1996)*. Reality Street, 2016.

bpNichol. *The Captain Poetry Poems*. Blew Ointment Press, 1970.

bpNichol. *Organ Music*. Black Moss Press, 2012.

C. E. Hubbard. *Grasses: A Guide to their Structure, Identification, Uses and Distribution in the British Isles*. Penguin, 1992.

Charlemagne Palestine. *Cathédrale de Strasbourg*. Erratum, 2016. LP.

David Bowie & Bing Crosby. *Peace On Earth/The Little Drummer Boy*. RCA. 1982. Single.

Dick Hyman. *The Man From O.R.G.A.N.* Command, 1965. LP.

Divine Euterpe: 13th-20th Century Organ Music by Women Composers. Kimberly Marshall at the Rosales Organ of Trinity Episcopal Cathedral, Portland, Oregon. Loft Recordings, 2000. CD.

Early Voyages and Travels in the Levant: The Diary of Master Thomas Dallam, 1599-1600. The Hakluyt Society, 1893.

18th Century English Organ Music. Margaret Phillips on the organ of St Matthew's Church, Westminster. Gamut Classics, 1990. CD.

Elton John. *Captain Fantastic & the Brown Dirt Cowboy*. MCA, 1975. LP.

Elton John. *Tiny Dancer*. UNI Records, 1972. Single.

Ethel Smith. *Lady Fingers*. Decca, 1958. LP.

Francis Routh. *Early English Organ Music from the Middle Ages to 1837*. Barrie & Jenkins, 1973

From Stanley to Wesley, Vols. 1-6. Jennifer Bate plays 18th Century Organ Music on Period Instruments at Adlington Hall, The Dolmetsch Collection, St Michael's Mount, Kenwood House, Killerton House & Everingham Chapel. Unicorn-Kanchana, 1990. 6XCD.

George Ashdown Audsley. *Organ Stops and their Artistic Registration*. The W. H. Gray Co., 1921.

Hannah Weiner. *Code Poems*, Station Hill, 1982.

Jacques Brel Chante La Belgique. Barclay, 1963. Compilation LP.

John Bull. *Ausgewählte Werke*. Gamben-Consort Johannes Koch; Susi Jeans, Virginal; Francis Cameron, Orgel. Archiv, 1968. LP.

John James. *A Theory of Poetry*. Street Editions, 1977.

John Norman. *The Box of Whistles: The History and Recent Development of Organ Case Design*. Society for Promoting Christian Knowledge, 2007.

Jonathan Gathorne-Hardy. *The Sultan's Organ: The Epic Voyage of Thomas Dallam and his extraordinary Musical Instrument to Constantinople in 1599 and his Time in the Palace and Harem of the Ottoman Sultan*. Propolis, 2017.

Joseph Beuys/Henning Christiansen. *Schottische Symphonie/Requiem of Art*. Edition Schellmann, 1973. LP.

Joseph Lanza. *Elevator Music: A Surreal History of Muzak, Easy-Listening and other Moodsong*. Quartet Books, 1995.

Ken White. *The Quaggy River and its Catchment Area*. Quaggy Action Waterways Group, 2012.

Klaus Wunderlich. *Hits Again 1-5*. Telefunken, 1971-1974. 5XLP.

Klaus Wunderlich. *Sound 2000: Moog, Organ, Rhythm*. Telefunken, 1973. LP.

L'age d'or de la musique d'orgue Anglaise. Kenneth Gilbert à l'orgue historique Dallam de Lanvellec. ADDA, 1989. CD.

Lauren Redhead/Alistair Zaldua. *Diapason: Music for Organ & Electronics*. SFZ Music, 2015. CD.

Marvin Gaye. *Midnight Love*. Columbia, 1982. LP.

Military Wives with Gareth Malone. *Wherever You Are*. Decca, 2011. Single.

Moondog. *Organ Rounds*. SMC Pro-Arte, 1950. Shellac 10".

More Sweet to Hear: Organs and Voices of Tudor England. Magnus Williamson, organ, with the Choir of Gonville and Caius College Cambridge, directed by Geoffrey Webber. OxRecs, 2011. CD.

Olivier Messiaen. *Messiaen par lui-même*. EMI Classics, 1992. 4XCD.

Paula Claire. *THE GREAT ORGAN: A Found Poem/Performance Text for Bob Cobbing on his 60th Birthday, 30 July 1980*. Writers Forum, 1982.

Piero Heliczer. *& I Dreamt I Shot Arrows in My Amazon Bra*. Dead Language/Matrix Press, 1961.

Power and Dunstaple: Masses and Motets. The Hilliard Ensemble. Warner Classics, 2012. CD.

Prince Far I. *Cry Tuff Dub Encounter Chapter 3.* Pressure Sounds, 1996. CD Reissue.

Renée & Renato. *Save Your Love.* Sonate, 1982. Single.

Soft Machine. *Third.* CBS, 1970. LP.

Soft Machine. *Fourth.* CBS, 1971. LP.

Stanford E. Lehmberg. *Cathedrals Under Siege: Cathedrals in English Society, 1600-1700.* University of Exeter Press, 1996.

Stephen Bicknell. *The History of the English Organ.* Cambridge University Press, 1996.

Stock, Hausen & Walkman. *Organ Transplants Vol. 1.* Hot Air, 1996. CD.

Stock, Hausen & Walkman. *Organ Transplants Vol. 2.* Hot Air, 2000. CD.

Supertramp. *Even in the Quietest Moments.* A&M Records, 1977. LP.

Supertramp. *Breakfast in America.* A&M Records, 1979. LP.

The Elusive English Organ. Feat. Daniel Moult. Fugue State Films, 2010. DVD.

The Eton Choirbook Collection. The Sixteen/Harry Christophers. The Sixteen Productions, 2003. 5XCDs.

The Fall. *Are You Are Missing Winner.* Remastered & expanded edition, Castle Music, 2006. CD.

The John Reading Manuscripts of Dulwich College. Riccardo Bonci at the 1760 George England organ in Christ's Chapel of God's Gift, Dulwich, London. Brilliant Classics, 2013. CD.

The Kinks. *Autumn Almanac.* Pye Records, 1967. Single.

The Maytals. *John James.* Randy's, 1964. Single.

The Soft Machine. *The Soft Machine.* ABC Probe, 1968. LP.

The Upsetters. *Return of the Super Ape.* Lion of Judah, 1978. LP.

Tudor Church Music from Durham Cathedral. Durham Cathedral Choir; Durham Cathedral Consort of Singers. Directed by James Lancelot. Keith Wright, organist. Featuring the Wetheringsett Organ. CD.

Twelve East Anglian Organs. Played by Geoffrey Hannant. Priory, 2005. Recordings made in 1977 and 1978. 2XCD.

Wang Chung. *Everybody Wang Chung Tonight: Wang Chung's Greatest Hits.* Geffen Records, 1997. Compilation CD.

Ziggy Stardust and the Spiders from Mars: The Motion Picture. Parlophone Records, 2003. DVD.

ACKNOWLEDGEMENTS

With many thanks to the editors of the following online and print publications within whose pages these poems have appeared:

Open Letter; VLAK; Painted, Spoken; For Simon Howard; PEEPSFEST: in celebration of Tommy Peeps/Linus Slug/all things Mendoza; Crater Press Broadside; Infinite Editions; Cambridge Literary Review; English: The Journal of the English Society; Fence; An Educated Desire: Robert Sheppard at 60; Dusie; Summer Stock; Poems in Which; Fugue and Subterfuge: A Festschrift for Alan Halsey; face down in the book of revelation: for Peter Hughes on his 60th Birthday; Other Room Anthology; Datableed; Tentacular; Erotoplasty.

A recital, what is a recital, it is an organ and use does not strengthen valor, it soothes medicine.

Gertrude Stein, Tender Buttons

I've heard an Organ talk, sometimes —
In a Cathedral Aisle,
And understood no word it said —
Yet held my breath, the while —

Emily Dickinson, "I've heard an organ talk, sometimes"

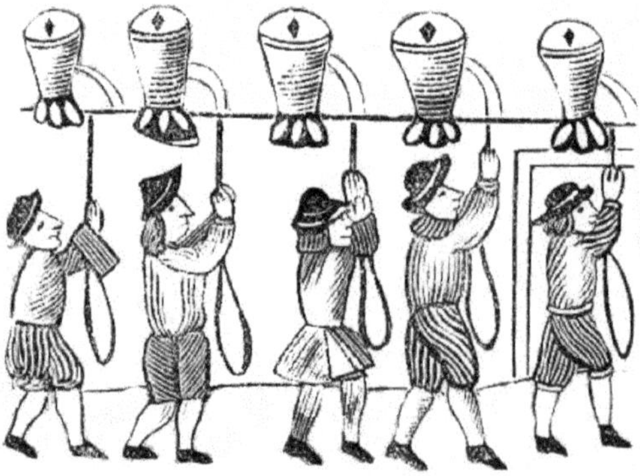